The night King Uther d
stirring, strode from Ti
lightning filled the dark
long ship appeared, shi
those who manned her.
Merlin descended with all speed
As they watched, a huge wave, its crest blazing with a dazzling light, broke on the shore and, as it retreated, a small babe was left on the sand. As Merlin gently picked him up he cried, 'Our King. An heir for Uther!'

Also in this series in Mayflower Books

Welsh Walks and Legends
by Showell Styles
(Illustrated)

J. H. N. Mason

West Country Walks and Legends

A MAYFLOWER BOOK

GRANADA

London Toronto Sydney New York

Published by Granada Publishing Limited
in 1980

ISBN 0 583 13228 6

A Mayflower UK Original

Granada Publishing Limited
Frogmore, St Albans, Herts AL2 2NF
and
3 Upper James Street, London W1R 4BP
866 United Nations Plaza, New York, NY 10017, USA
117 York Street, Sydney, NSW 2000, Australia
100 Skyway Avenue, Rexdale, Ontario, M9W 3A6, Canada
PO Box 84165, Greenside, 2034 Johannesburg, South Africa
61 Beach Road, Auckland, New Zealand

Set, printed and bound in Great Britain by
Cox & Wyman Ltd, Reading
Filmset in Linotype Plantin

CONTENTS

INTRODUCTION

This is a collection of Legends from the West Country with Walks in the area where they took place or may have taken place. There is a wealth of legend in the West, all bearing the stamp of the landscape from which they are drawn: those from the rock-strewn moors of Cornwall and Devon have a touch of the eerie and demonic; in those of the cliffs and raging seas there are shipwrecks, dangerous mermaids and smugglers. I hope you will find them all a satisfying contribution to your enjoyment of one of Britain's finest regions.

I have been fortunate in having Robert Hunt's classic *Popular Romances of the West of England*, written nearly a hundred years ago, from which to draw many Cornish legends. The Arthurian stories 'The Coming of Arthur' and 'Gareth and Lynette' are based on Tennyson's *Idylls of the King*. There are of course many versions of the King Arthur, Tristan and Isolde and other Legends and here I follow the lead of Showell Styles in his *Welsh Walks and Legends* by saying I have selected those I like best. In some instances the subjects are actual people who became 'living legends' in their time; this adds, I think, to the interest of the stories. Other sources from which I have had great help are listed in the Bibliography and are recommended for those who wish to delve deeper into the stories.

The Walks are planned to bring you back to the starting point, chosen as a convenient spot for parking a car. They are suitable in most cases for all tastes and abilities. Where a route is not suited to the elderly or young children under eight there is a note to that effect. For those without a car, at the end of each walk-description there is information regarding convenient bus services, if they exist, but it is always necessary to check locally the bus time-table, preferably some time before the intended walk as the times and days of operation are liable to alteration. The Legends and Walks are grouped under areas: a sketch-map on pp. 184–5 will help you locate each one. The Grid Reference on the Ordnance Survey 1:50,000 maps of the starting point of each Walk is given in the text. The first three figures of the reference denote the number of the Ordnance Survey map.

No special boots or clothing are required for the Walks but good comfortable walking shoes should be worn. Ladies should avoid wearing high heels as they could be dangerous, especially on the Coast Paths. Take adequate rainwear. The times given for the Walks are based on a moderate pace and do not allow for stops en route, whether to enjoy the view or to eat your picnic.

All the Walks are routed over public rights-of-way as shown on the Ordnance Survey 1:50,000 maps at the time of writing. One or two 'permissive paths' are also used. No responsibility can be borne for subsequent alterations which may affect the Walks. Always keep strictly to the indicated paths. When walking along roads, keep in single file close to the side of the road and facing oncoming traffic. Dogs should be kept on a lead where there are sheep or cattle. Close all gates and leave no litter.

NORTH DEVON AND SOMERSET

The Legend of Glastonbury

Gareth and Lynette

Lorna Doone

Glenthorne and the Legend of Joseph of Arimathea

THE LEGEND OF GLASTONBURY

To the traveller catching sight from a distance, for the first time, of the 500-ft hill, Glastonbury Tor, surmounted by its chapel, rising solitary from the plains of Somerset, the effect is striking. The town of Glastonbury below the Tor with the majestic ruined Abbey and other links with the earliest days of Christianity in Britain completes the picture of one of the West Country's most dramatic sites.

Glastonbury in many ways provides mysteries which may never be solved. Nevertheless its impact on the life of Britain has been deep and far-reaching; in the times before the Norman Conquest, the influence of the monastery under men like St Dunstan was immense and its claim to be the first Christian community in the Kingdom gave it unique prestige. The story of Glastonbury's growth is part legend, part authentic history. Here, firstly, are the facts.

The Abbey was part of a large monastery and the ruins you see today are of the Great Church, built to replace the one burnt down in 1184. Not only was the early church destroyed in this fire but also the rest of the monastery, with its possessions, including, unfortunately, documents and manuscripts which, if they had survived, might have filled the gaps in our story. The new church was ready in 1213 and stood until it was destroyed in the Dissolution of the Monasteries in 1539 and the stones used for buildings in the town.

The earliest recorded structure on the site of the monastery was one of wattle and daub, the Old Church, discovered, after he had conquered Somerset, by the Saxon King of Wessex, Ine, who ruled 688–726. Obviously impressed by the community he presented them with endowments to increase their income and built a new stone church. The sites of these early buildings and the early cemetery were on the west side of the Great Church. The first stone church was enlarged by St Dunstan, Abbot of Glastonbury 940–960,

Glastonbury Tor. *(Edmund Swinglehurst)*

before he became Archbishop of Canterbury. Dunstan undertook this work, as well as the monastic buildings, as the result of a dream in which an angel foretold he would become abbot of a great monastery and rebuild it. It was said of Dunstan that when he was at Glastonbury he was tempted by the Devil in the guise of a beautiful woman. Dunstan's reaction was to seize the 'lady's' nose in a pair of tongs which caused a quick retreat! After 1066, under the Normans, two successive churches were erected on the site of the present ruined Great Church; they also constructed the cloister and adjacent accommodation for the monks. It was the last of the early Norman buildings which was destroyed in the great fire of 1184.

These then, very roughly, are the verifiable stages of the monastery's existence from the eighth century onwards. Who was responsible for starting the community round the Old Church of wattle and daub found by King Ine and when did this happen? It is here that all we have to fall back on are legends, some credible, many fanciful. Some of these legends put forward the claim that Christ's disciples first brought the Gospel to Glastonbury; others, that St Patrick and the early Fathers of the Celtic Church were the founders of the community.

The most reliable account of Glastonbury's earliest days is that of the historian, William of Malmesbury, who in about 1130 visited the Abbey to gather material for a history of Britain he was writing. He set down what he had learned in a *History of Glastonbury's Antiquities*, but his original manuscript has been lost. The later copies all contain alterations by the monks themselves, giving earlier dates of foundation than William does, adding many fanciful details. Why we know the main contents of William's first manuscript is because he incorporated his Glastonbury notes in his subsequent work, *History of the Kings of England*, which has survived.

William recounts how he was told at the Abbey that an early King of the Britons, Lucius, sent to Pope Eleutherius (about 174–89) for missionaries to come to Britain: that the Pope sent them and they settled in Glastonbury, building its first church. William implies, however, that no reliable evidence was presented to him on this. He then mentions two stone monuments near the Old Church which he examined. These gave the names of past Abbots and other saints, many of whom had lived and died in Glastonbury and who were buried there. These included St Patrick who, after the conversion of the Irish, became Abbot and died in 472. Others who spent some time at the Abbey were St David, St Bridget and St Benignus (to whom one of Glastonbury's parish churches is dedicated).

It was after about 1250 that versions of William of Malmesbury's book on Glastonbury began to circulate with 'fabricated' additions covering most of the present-day legends. These stories assert that in the year 63, St Philip, one of the original disciples, after bringing the Gospel to Gaul sent a mission of twelve disciples, led by St Joseph of

Arimathea* to Britain. They were given a site by the pagan king and this was Glastonbury. When they died the place became deserted until the missionaries from Pope Eleutherius arrived, now given the names Phaganus and Deruvianus, who converted Britain, dying at Glastonbury where their bones still rested. An alleged 'charter' of St Patrick of 430 was then quoted at length, telling how the saint found twelve hermits when he arrived at Glastonbury and took one of them, Wellias, to the top of the Tor where they found a ruined chapel with a book containing the acts of Phaganus and Deruvianus. Patrick then decreed that the hermits should rebuild the chapel of St Michael on the Tor and the two bodies should reside there.

Many details were then given of the lives at Glastonbury of SS David, Columba, Bridget, Paulinus, Gildas, all of whom died and had their tombs and relics there. All these invented stories served to enhance the attractions of Glastonbury as a place of pilgrimage and pilgrims flocked from all parts to worship at the shrines of the saints. Meanwhile, another figure appeared in the story, and this appearance did more than anything else to add to the aura of greatness surrounding the Abbey – the association of King Arthur with Glastonbury. During the first half of the twelfth century, the priest Geoffrey of Monmouth, of Welsh and Norman ancestry, brought out his *History of the Kings of Britain*, with a view perhaps to glorifying the Celtic element in the kingdom. In this book are recounted the fabulous exploits of the hero King Arthur and his Knights. Victorious in battle; defending the weak against the strong; courtly love where lives are risked for a lady's favours – all these expressed the romance of the age and soon Geoffrey's book was the rage of all literate circles not only in Britain but also on the Continent. The announcement in 1191 that the grave of Arthur and his queen

*The story of St Joseph of Arimathea and his journey to Britain with the Holy Grail is recounted on pp. 34–6, *Glenthorne and the Legend of St Joseph of Arimathea*.

Guinevere had been found at Glastonbury caused a sensation. Deep down in the earth near the old cemetery in the Abbey grounds, diggers had come across two skeletons: one of an extremely tall and well-built man and the other of a golden-haired woman. Both skeletons were lying in the remains of an oaken dug-out canoe. Nearby was found a small stone cross with a Latin inscription reading when translated: 'Here lies buried the famous King Arthur, in the Isle of Avalon'. The cross existed. The antiquary Camden handled and made a drawing of it in 1607.

There were two startling deductions from the discovery of the grave: Arthur's actual death and burial had previously never been mentioned in the legends. He had been reckoned to be immortal and would return to save his nation in time of need. Secondly, the location of the Isle of Avalon where he had been taken, wounded, after his defeat by Modred had only been conjecture and here it was identified with Glastonbury! In the next century the remains were transferred with all pomp and ceremony to a new tomb in the Great Church in the presence of Edward I and his Queen. This tomb was destroyed at the Dissolution. Was the 'discovery' of the remains of Arthur and Guinevere staged with the object in mind of raising funds to help meet the vastly increased expense of rebuilding after the fire of 1184? R. F. Treharne in his *The Glastonbury Legends* gives good reasons why this could very well have been the case.

Although the legends of the founding of Glastonbury will not stand up to scientific scrutiny, there still remain questions to be answered. Who had been responsible for founding the Christian community King Ine came across in the seventh century? It was undoubtedly a Celtic Christian cell and could have been founded, if not by St Patrick, then possibly by other Celtic missionaries from either Ireland, Wales or Brittany as had been established in Cornwall. Why was Glastonbury first chosen? C. A. Ralegh Radford in the excellent colour booklet *Glastonbury Abbey, Isle of Avalon*, in the Pitkin Pride of Britain series, mentions a theory that 'Ponter's Ball', a high Iron Age earthwork 2 miles east of the Abbey on the A361, erected when Glastonbury was an island (the Bristol Channel formerly penetrated many miles inland forming shallow creeks and swamps), could have been the wall of a pagan Celtic sanctuary. It would have been natural to replace this by a Christian place of worship. Close to Glastonbury and at Meare, 4 miles to the north-west, are the traces of the famous lake-villages of 50 BC. Evidence of a surprisingly high standard of life and culture could indicate that the area was of importance since before the Roman occupation, although there are few signs of Roman settlement. As far as Arthurian legend is concerned it is generally accepted that Arthur typifies some Roman-British hero who resisted the Germanic invaders. Recent excavations at Cadbury Castle, the extensive Iron Age hill-fort only 12 miles away, have disclosed evidence of use as a powerful stronghold after the Roman occupation. This suggests it might have been the site of one of Arthur's victories over the Saxons. Another Arthurian legend is that Guinevere was abducted by King Malwas of Somerset and imprisoned on Tor Hill, to be freed by Arthur. Excavations on Tor Hill indicate a possible post-Roman signal station.

With modern aids to scientific archaeology and research, yesterday's legends may well be shown to be today's historical facts. Maybe one day the key to the Glastonbury Legends may be found.

THE WALK:
CIRCULAR WALK WITH STEEP ASCENT OF TOR HILL. WALK CAN BE REARRANGED FOR A LESS STEEP CLIMB

MAP SQUARE I3
O.S. reference: 183/501390
Allow 1½ hours' walking time. Suitable for Under Eights. The elderly might find the steep climb up the Tor beyond their powers. They should manage the alternative.

The Glastonbury Information Centre is at 7 Northload Street, running north from the Market Cross in the centre of the town. There you can be advised of the best way to spend your time and get brochures, maps, etc.

It is assumed that you will have visited the Abbey, the Tribunal, St John's Church and other historical sites in the town and now wish to see some of the surroundings. The Walk starts from the 'top' (east end) of the High Street, the main street of the town. There are a number of car parks in Glastonbury including one in Silver Street, running just behind (south) and parallel to the top end of the High Street. For the Walk turn right out of the High Street down Lambrook Street (A361) continuing as Chilkwell Street, running along the east boundary of the Abbey grounds. Turn left up Dod Lane to a stile leading to a footpath above Bushy Combe, a pleasant area with trees. Cross the next stile and keep straight on along the road for a few yards then over another stile to a path. This brings you to a lane (Wellhouse Lane). Carry straight on at the junction down Stone Down Lane. A short way on your right is the start of the steep path up the Tor. On the summit is the tower, all that is left of the fourteenth-century chapel of St Michael. Extensive views in all directions (the Information Centre has a small descriptive leaflet of the views). Return from the top by the well-trod path down the gentler slope. Turn left at the bottom into Chilkwell Street. Turn right and on your right is Chalice Well. This is the legendary spring where Joseph of Arimathea is said to have hidden the Holy Grail. It can be visited March–October. After Chalice Well, continue right along Chilkwell Street (A361) and it will bring you back in about ½-mile to the top of High Street.

For the alternative easier ascent of the Tor, reverse the Walk, keeping straight down Chilkwell Street to Chalice Well. Turn left for a few yards up Wellhouse Lane taking the footpath you will see leading up the Tor. Return the same way.

The above routes are based on Walk 1 in *Glastonbury Footpath*

Walks published by the Glastonbury Conservation Society. Highly recommended for further walks.

Glastonbury is linked by bus with Bridgwater, Taunton, Wells, Yeovil, etc.

GARETH AND LYNETTE

Gareth, tall and fair, youngest son of King Lot of Orkney and his Queen, Bellicent, sister of King Arthur, sat moping at his father's castle. Why, he asked himself for the hundredth time, would his mother not let him join his brothers, Gawain and Modred, at Arthur's court and take his place among the knights? Why should he not be able to range himself alongside them to prove his manhood in the fight for the right? Why should he have to sit day after day, bored to tears, by the fireside or chase over the hills after defenceless deer or hares, when he longed for more worthy game: Arthur's foes? Had he not, when his brothers were at home, often unseated Gawain in the trial jousts they used to have? True, his father, King Lot, severely wounded after an ill-advised revolt against Arthur, now lay a sick man, paralysed, awaiting death, but that made it all the more necessary for him to prove to Arthur that he would be as true to him as the steel of Excalibur, the King's sword.

Once more he pleaded with Bellicent who, seeing his determination, gave her consent at last but, in order to break his resolve, imposed a harsh condition. 'Go,' she said, 'but promise me you will disguise yourself and serve for a year and a day in the kitchens of Camelot as a scullion, without revealing who you are.' To her chagrin, this did not deter Gareth and he readily swore he would carry out his mother's wish and, assuming a lowly disguise, set out for Arthur's court. It was spring and the countryside was at its loveliest as he came after many days in sight of the magic Camelot, its towers and spires seeming to dance in the morning mist with the early sun tingeing them with gleams of dazzling light. Lost in wonder he made his way to the Palace where the King was receiving those who had a petition, as was the custom each morning. After watching with awe the King delivering judgement Gareth pressed forward and asked that he should be allowed to serve his majesty in the humblest position – a scullion in the kitchen, but without revealing his name. Arthur granted the request and handed him over to the care of Sir Kay, the surly steward.

Sir Kay, seeming to detect something noble about his new kitchen-boy, took a dislike to him, setting him always the dirtiest and most menial tasks – scouring the greasiest utensils, chopping wood in the wettest weather, cleaning out the sootiest flues. Gareth carried out all these tasks cheerfully and well. What delighted him was the occasional chance to listen to the other lads telling tales of his heroes, Sir Lancelot and the other knights. He also enjoyed the rough games they played in which he more than held his own. After a month he received some glad news: Queen Bellicent repented of the harsh condition she had imposed on her son and had sent one of her squires with a release from his promise and a magnificent suit of armour. Overjoyed, Gareth ran to the King and, revealing who he was, begged to be allowed to enrol as one of his knights, in secret, if need be, until he had proved himself. 'In secret?' said Arthur, 'Yea, but my truest knight, Sir Lancelot, must know.'

As he spoke, a fair, haughty maiden strode into the hall and with flashing eyes accused the King of letting parts of his kingdom lapse into disorder, demanding that Sir Lancelot should be sent to aid her sister. She declared her name was Lynette and that her sister, Lyonors, was besieged in her home, Castle Perilous, by four evil knights, brothers, three of whom guarded the three river crossings on the approaches to the Castle. The fourth was laying siege to the Castle itself until Lyonors promised to marry him. The three called themselves Morning Star, Noon Sun and Evening Star; the fourth, always clad in black armour emblazoned with a white skull, was Night.

Gareth, still in his scullion clothes, beseeched the King to send him on this quest. Arthur hesitated and then assented. Lynette was much displeased. 'I asked for the greatest of your knights and you send this kitchen-boy!' she cried and swept out of the King's presence, mounted her horse and galloped away. Gareth followed and, running to the gate of the Palace, found awaiting him a marvellous war-horse with all accoutrements, a gift from the King. Throwing off his kitchen clothes he put on his armour and taking his lance hurried after Lynette, unaware that Arthur had ordered Lancelot to follow them secretly. After a hard ride he caught up with the maiden who, as he drew alongside, cried, 'What are you doing here? If the King is not willing to send Sir Lancelot to help my sister he could at least choose one of his other knights and not his evil-smelling kitchen-knave!' 'Whatever you say,' answered Gareth, 'I will finish this quest or die.' And as Lynette spurred her horse on its way, he followed her at a distance.

Soon the river came into view and, on the other side of the bridge, the splendid tents of Sir Morning Star. At Gareth's approach he shouted a challenge to which Lynette answered that his opponent was not Lancelot but one of Arthur's kitchen-slaves. With a roar the knight called for his armour and three lovely maidens appeared and helped him to put it on. Calling out insults he rode at Gareth who, levelling his lance, advanced to meet him. They clashed in the centre of the bridge and so great was the shock they were both unhorsed. Gareth was first on his feet and with a mighty blow from his sword, brought the other to his knees. 'Shall I kill or spare him?' he asked of Lynette. 'You have no right to kill one nobler than yourself!' she cried. 'Free him!' 'Go back to Camelot,' said Gareth to the knight, 'and tell Arthur his kitchen-boy has triumphed and spared you,' and he and Lynette rode on.

'You smell a little sweeter now,' said the maiden, 'but I despise you all the more. You will have a harder task with the next one.' They then came to where the knight Noon Sun was waiting by the river to challenge Gareth and straightaway dashed at him, the bright sun flashing on his shield. They met in mid-stream in a dreadful collision, aiming blows at each other. Noon Sun's horse slipped and was carried away by the stream. The rider surrendered and pleaded for mercy. Gareth spared him and sent him on his way to Arthur for his judgement. 'Now do you think I have a chance of freeing your sister?' he asked Lynette. 'His horse stumbled on a rock. You were lucky,' she replied.

On to the next bend in the river and there stood by the bridge the eldest brother, Evening Star, clad in skins over which he quickly donned his armour, calling out in defiance. 'The youth has overcome your brother,' cried Lynette, 'and will vanquish you!' Gareth smiled to himself at this, her first encouraging word, and rushed to meet the knight on the bridge where they exchanged the hardest blows for which they could muster strength. Gareth broke the other's sword and the knight then grappled with him. They swayed together, utterly exhausted, trying to find a fatal hold, then, with a mighty effort, Gareth toppled Evening Star into the river where his armour trapped him.

As they rode on for the final test, Lynette said, 'Sir Knight – I will call you kitchen-knave no more. I am ashamed that I have treated you so and ask your pardon.' Answered Gareth: 'He is no true knight who is deterred by a lady's waywardness from his duty – gladly I forgive you.' 'There is a cave nearby where my sister has had provisions set. Let us go there and refresh ourselves,' she said.

They found the cave and entered. Lancelot who had been following, drawing ever nearer, crept into the cave behind them and challenged Gareth who turned and closed with the stranger. He was no match for him and was soon stretched on his back on the ground. Lancelot helped him to his feet and revealed his identity. Gareth's joy at meeting Arthur's champion was tinged with shame at being so easily put on his back, but he recovered when Lancelot told him how many times he himself had been the loser. Lynette had been watching this with growing anger. 'What is this trick that has been played on me?' she cried. 'I am sick of you both.' 'Nay,' replied Lancelot, 'Gareth is a true knight, worthy to join me at the Round Table – he has been sorely tested and has triumphed. Now he must meet his last adversary.'

They came to Castle Perilous and from a magnificent black pavilion came the fearsome figure of Night, on a black charger, both in black armour, the rider's with a white skull emblazoned. Gareth, his heart beating fast and his mouth dry, rode at him and with one blow of his sword struck off the black helmet, revealing the face of a young boy who surrendered and cried out for pardon. He told how his brothers had forced him to play the role to frighten the Lady Lyonors while they hoped to entice Lancelot to come to her rescue. They could then kill him and revenge themselves for some grievance.

Lancelot pardoned him and the two knights freed the Lady of Castle Perilous. The next days were filled with feasting and revelling in which, however, Lynette did not seem whole-heartedly to join. Perhaps she still felt she had somehow been the victim of a trick. Some say she eventually married Gareth; others say he wed Lyonors. I think it must have been Lyonors.

THE WALK:
ROUND CADBURY CASTLE,
HILL-FORT AND POSSIBLE
SITE OF CAMELOT

MAP SQUARE J3
O.S. reference: 183/632255
A short walk up to the crest and round the ramparts. Allow 1 hour. Suitable for all ages.

Cadbury Castle, a large hill-fort of Iron Age origin (about 700 BC), which may be Arthur's Camelot, lies ½-mile south of the main A303 road. Take the turning 2 miles east of Sparkford signposted SOUTH CADBURY. You should be able to park your car by the roadside in this small village. Prominent is the thirteenth-century church of St Thomas à Becket which is well worth a visit. Continuing south past the church there is on the right between a thatched cottage and a stone house, Castle Keep, the start of a trackway, with a notice headed CADBURY/CAMELOT, leading up to the summit of Cadbury Castle, an extensive wooded hill dominating the village. Opposite the entrance of the trackway is an attractive thatched stone-built farmhouse bearing the date 1687.

The first part of the trackway up to the Castle site is likely to be a little muddy if there has been any rain. After a short climb you come to where the track cuts through the embankment constructed on the crest of the hill forming the north-east entrance to the stronghold. As you emerge on to the flat summit you will see to the right and the left the bank running round the summit of the hill, the remains of the foundations of the palisades. The bank extends for nearly a mile and you can walk around enjoying the splendid views over the countryside, including Glastonbury Tor, 12 miles to the north-west. On the south side of the hill you will see clearly the impressive system of high banks and deep ditches, carved from the rock and supported by masonry in places, making the fortress difficult to subdue even in the present day. There are also entrances in the south-west and north-west of the area.

The need for a thorough excavation of Cadbury Castle was sparked off through the chance discovery by a visitor some years ago of a fragment of sixth-century Mediterranean pottery. This indicated the possibility of an important settlement on the site in the Dark Ages, after the Romans had left the country. As the fragment could have been from a wine-jar this would justify the theory that the inhabitants could have been wealthy enough to use wine imported from abroad. The 1966–70 excavations did in fact confirm the occupation in Arthurian (sixth century) times and a series of post-holes proved there could have been a large feasting-hall. There was also evidence of the existence of other rooms. Apart from the Arthurian remains, the excavators discovered traces of a massacre of Britons on the site by the Romans in about AD 70, possibly when resisting re-settlement. The whole fascinating story of the excavations is recounted by the leader of the team, Leslie Alcock, in his book By South Cadbury that is

Camelot. *Cadbury Castle could very well have been the stronghold used by Arthur, or some other heroic leader, as his base for a successful resistance against the barbarian Saxon invaders.*

There is a bus service on Fridays and Saturdays between Bruton and Yeovil (Brutonian Bus Co) which calls at South Cadbury. The inn, The Red Lion, serves food in the summer.

LORNA DOONE

Everyone who visits Exmoor has heard of Lorna Doone but I suspect that not very many have read R. D. Blackmore's novel written in 1869 of which the beautiful Lorna is the heroine. Although rather long and in a style which seems wordy nowadays it is a good yarn, well worth reading – especially if you are spending your holidays near Exmoor. The setting is in the north part of the moor just below County Gate; here the Badgworthy Water (pronounced Badgery) joins the Lyn River. Two and a half miles farther south is the area where traditionally the Doone family of robbers had their hideout.

The narrator and hero is Jan Ridd, a giant of a man, farmer and wrestling champion, living in the village of Oare near County Gate. Here is an outline of the romance.

Jan tells how in 1673 as a boy of 12 he lost his farmer father who was robbed and killed by the Doones on his way home from Porlock market and how, shortly after, while exploring the Badgworthy valley he meets a beautiful young girl who tells him she is Lorna Doone. Seven years later, not being able to dismiss Lorna from his mind, he penetrates the fastness of the Doones and again finds Lorna, now a lovely young woman, and falls in love with her. At a later secret meeting she tells him that she regards old Sir Ensor Doone, head of the Doones, as her grandfather, but that a young Scottish nobleman, Alan Brandir, came to Doone Gate and claimed he was her guardian. He was challenged by Carver Doone, Sir Ensor's rascally son, and in a sword fight was killed by him.

Sir Ensor dies and Carver wants to marry Lorna who refuses him and is locked up by him in a house in the valley. Jan Ridd finds her and releases her, taking her to his farm, Parson's Barrow, at Oare, where she is welcomed into the family circle by his mother and his sisters, Annie and Lizzie.

Malmsmead – Lorna Doone Farm. *(Edmund Swinglehurst)*

The authorities send armed men under a Captain Jeremy Stickles against the Doones but they run into an ambush. The Devon and Somerset men, after coming to blows among themselves, beat an ignominious retreat. During one of Jan's absences from the farm Lorna is sent for by the Court of Chancery in London and, as the Lady Lorna Dugal, is put in the care of her uncle, the Earl of Loch Awe, who lives in Kensington.

Jan's sister Annie marries a cousin, a reformed highwayman, Tom Faggus, who goes off to join the Duke of Monmouth's rebellion. Jan Ridd quixotically responds to his sister's plea to go after him and bring him back but he finds himself caught up in the Battle of Sedgemoor. He finds Tom who is wounded. Unfortunately he himself is caught by Kirke's Lambs, King James's cruel troopers, but is providentially saved from hanging by Captain Stickle.

Jan nevertheless has to go to London to answer charges of being a rebel. While in London he manages to get in touch with Lorna. She had written many letters to him but her maid, Gwenny, from a misplaced sense of duty, had destroyed them instead of giving them to the messenger. The two lovers renew their vows but Lorna's position seems to be a barrier to their marrying. Jan Ridd is able to save the Earl's life by overcoming and capturing three thieves who break into his house in Kensington. As a Scottish Catholic the Earl is well placed at Court and Lorna has come under the notice of the Queen. Jan is knighted by the King for having saved the Earl's life but returns to the farm with little hope of marrying Lorna.

After a series of horrible outrages by the Doones, another attack on their stronghold is mounted which Jan is asked to lead. This time the attempt is successful and the Doones are all killed or captured and their settlement destroyed. Carver Doone, however, escapes.

The Earl dies and by paying a large sum Lorna is freed from Chancery, the King giving his consent to her marriage to Jan. During the wedding service in Oare Church a shot is fired from a window and Lorna is hit. Jan chases after the culprit, Carver Doone, and corners him on a marshy tract of the moor. A desperate sword fight ensues and Carver falls and is swallowed up in the bog. Jan is severely wounded but he and Lorna are both nursed back to health. Sir Jan and his lady settle down to married bliss.

The foregoing summary omits many characters and sub-plots: Jan's Uncle Rueben Huckaback of Dulverton and his daughter Ruth who loves Jan secretly and the uncle's attempt to mine gold on the moor; Jan's neighbours, the Snowes, who hope their daughter will marry Jan (the Snowes actually lived in the area and have a monument in Oare Church); Judge Jeffreys and so on; but it gives some idea of the story.

Whether the Doone family ever existed has been a matter of controversy for more than a hundred years. There seems to be no documentary or other reliable evidence of their existence but the tradition is a tremendously strong one.

Blackmore heard stories of them from a grandfather who had been Vicar of Oare in the early 1800s and there are many references to them in guidebooks on Exmoor from the 1830s onwards. A clergyman was shown in 1840 a long gun at Yenworthy Farm with which the wife of the farmer is said to have repulsed a Doone raid, as recounted in *Lorna Doone*. The family were said to have lived in the early 1600s and to have terrorized the neighbourhood, raiding farms and stealing cattle and sheep. The wild, lonely but fascinating stretches of moorland would certainly have encouraged such crimes, as those who explore the Doone Country will discover.

THE WALKS:
HERE ARE THREE WALKS IN THE LORNA DOONE COUNTRY:

1 FROM MALMSMEAD TO THE DOONE VALLEY, RETURNING THE SAME WAY
2 AS (1) TO THE DOONE VALLEY, RETURNING OVER THE MOOR
3 A SHORT WALK TO THE TOP OF DUNKERY BEACON

MAP SQUARE F2
O.S. references:
1 and 2: 180/792478
3: 181/904420

1: allow 1½ hours each way (5 miles)
2: allow 3½ hours (6½ miles)
3: allow 30 minutes each way

Suitable for all ages. Walk 1 can be shortened if desired.

WALKS 1 AND 2: *To explore the Doone Valley the best jumping-off place is Malmsmead, reached by a steep, narrow road near County Gate on the A39 between Lynmouth and Minehead. As you descend this road you see below Oare Church where Lorna was shot and the wooded valley of the East Lyn river into which flows Badgworthy Water. There is good parking space at Malmsmead also refreshment facilities, including pre-packed picnics. East of Oare Church is Oareford Farm which could have been Plover's*

Barrow, Jan Ridd's home. A John Ridd was churchwarden of Oare Church 1914–25. Parsonage Farm, between the church and Malmsmead, is where Blackmore used to stay.

The village of Oare. (*Exmoor National Park Dept., Somerset County Council*)

WALK I: *Turn left out of the car park; you then have two optional paths to start your walk to the Doone Valley: ahead you will see the Lorna Doone Riding Stables and a notice: PATH TO THE FAMOUS DOONE VALLEY and SHORT CUT TO DOONE VALLEY. Here you pay a small fee to use the path through the riding stables and along the bank of Badgworthy Water. The alternative (free) route starts on the road sloping up to the right of the riding stables. A short way along this road is a gate marked PUBLIC BRIDLEWAY TO DOONE VALLEY 2 MILES and a yellow waymark. Go through this gate (closing it after you) and follow this path, which soon drops down to the stream, joining the other path near the bridge at Cloud Farm (teas in the summer).*

The valley widens here and the clear stream runs musically over its rocky bed. You pass a memorial to Blackmore and then enter shady woods, full of bird song in the spring. Birds to be seen in spring and summer by the stream include redstart, grey wagtail and dipper. Before you emerge from the woods you cross a footbridge over a small stream (Lank Combe) where it enters Badgworthy Water. A little way up Lank Combe the stream flows over a series of smooth rocks in the form of 'steps'. These may have given Blackmore the idea of the dangerous Water Slide on the main river which guarded the Doones' fastness.

From the woods the valley opens out and here you are on the borders of the Doone territory, we are told. After walking for about 1½ hours from the start there is a junction of paths with a sign showing the directions to Exford, Brendon Common and Malmsmead. The stream joining the Badgworthy Water here is Hoccombe Water and the path to Brendon Common follows the Hoccombe Valley for ½-mile. It is along this stretch where, the experts tell us, the Doones had their dwellings; an investigator reports he has found traces of a number of houses. The track certainly widens to road-width and there are the ruins of a cottage, presumably later than the Doones' era. In any case, this lower Hoccombe Valley is a delightful spot for a rest or picnic. Return to Malmsmead the same way; you can, of course, shorten this walk as you wish.

WALK 2: *This is the same route outward as* WALK 1 *but returns over the Moor to Malmsmead allowing an experience of the attraction of these bare, windswept heights, so well described by Blackmore. Turn up the Brendon Common path from the signpost and continue past the reputed Doone hideout. The track, well used by horse-riders, is clear; there are one or two gates and helpful yellow waymarks. In autumn the bracken and purple heather are a wonderful sight. Climbing gradually you notice that even the bracken and heather fall away leaving only dank grass – not surprising as you are over 1200 ft above sea level. In some mud patches there may be deer tracks.*

After what seems to be the highest point on the path it begins to run along the southern crest of a valley, soon dropping in a curve to cross a stream (Lankcombe Ford). On the summit of the slope the other side is a signpost showing directions to Brendon, Doone Valley (where you have come from), Brendon Common and Malmsmead. Follow the Malmsmead track. In about 20 minutes you drop down to cross a rivulet, joining a wide sandy track on the other side. As this track climbs you get, in clear weather, marvellous views across the Bristol Channel to the Welsh coast as well as a bird's-eye view of Porlock Bay and the fertile Porlock Vale. Before long you come to a metalled road; cross straight over to a metal gate with a PUBLIC BRIDLEWAY sign to Malmsmead. Through this gate and straight in front is a rutted grass track running at right angles to the power line. Make for this and continue ahead; after a dip the bridleway enters Southern Wood, eventually swinging to the right down to Malmsmead opposite the car park.

WALK 3: *This short walk to the top of Dunkery Beacon (1704 ft) is not so strenuous as it sounds, as your starting point on the road is over 1400 ft above sea level. The road runs south from Allerford on the A39 to near Wheddon Cross on the B3224. Coming from Allerford, drive on until the road levels out after climbing. There are plenty of parking-spaces – the car park itself is a fine viewpoint (if you approach from the south, from the Wheddon Cross direction, do not stop at Dunkery Gate by the cattle-grid – unless you need stiff exercise – as the path from here to the top of the Beacon is steeper than from the main parking area 1 mile farther on).*

The path to the Beacon is clearly signposted from the car park and provides a gradual climb. From the summit you have the finest possible panorama of Exmoor and beyond – moor, wooded valleys and the Bristol Channel. Although you will undoubtedly choose a clear sunny day for your walk you may be able to conjure up the eerie scene when the young Jan Ridd riding on his pony over the Moor from his school in Tavistock to his home, after his father had been killed by the Doones, catches sight of the raiders riding through the mist, by the light of the Beacon, lit by them to guide them back to their valley.

There is a bus service on weekdays June–September between Minehead and Lynmouth, calling at County Gate. There is a short but steep bridleway from County Gate down to Malmsmead. In May the bus service runs on Monday's and Wednesdays only.

GLENTHORNE AND THE LEGEND OF JOSEPH OF ARIMATHEA

As mentioned in 'The Legend of Glastonbury' on pages 11–16, St Joseph of Arimathea was one of those credited with the founding of the first Christian settlement in Britain. Joseph was the rich Jew who, we are told in all the four gospels, went to Pontius Pilate, the Roman Governor of Judaea, after Christ's crucifixion, asking to be allowed to take away his body for burial. His request was granted and after having the body anointed with myrrh and aloes and draped in a winding-sheet, he laid him in a rock tomb which he had newly carved for himself. He was apparently a member of the Sanhedrin (Council), the supreme legal Jewish Authority who, even under the Romans, were allowed to exercise their function, apart from imposing the death penalty which duty was reserved for the Roman Governor. Joseph opposed the Council's condemnation of Jesus and was in fact a secret disciple. We are also told he was a friend of Nicodemus who 'came to Jesus by night' and that Nicodemus helped him with Jesus's burial.

The request to Pilate was more significant than the bare account suggests. The *Encyclopaedia Britannica* points out that Joseph's action not only identified him as a sympathizer of Jesus's but that he defied the Council by entombing him according to Jewish ritual when according to the law he was only entitled to a criminal's grave. This may have lost Joseph his seat on the Council. The courageous stand supports the tradition that he subsequently joined the disciples. The apocryphal 'Acts of Pilate' says he was imprisoned by the Council and miraculously released. Also that Pilate gave him the Holy Grail, the chalice used by Jesus at the Last Supper. Another story tells how he collected some of Jesus's blood in two 'cruets' or vials.

Joseph appears in the medieval account of an evangelization mission of the apostle Philip to Gaul. He was said to be one of the band of disciples who accompanied Philip, and after the conversion of Gaul had been completed he was sent in AD 63 to these islands to win the Britons for Christianity. With twelve companions he set sail and after many adventures landed on the coast of what we know now as North Devon. One of the possible landing places of Joseph and his fellow missionaries has been identified as Glenthorne beach on the border between Devon and Somerset and this is where we are suggesting a walk. Carrying the Holy Grail with them the little band started to make their way inland. Climbing up from the beach they became very thirsty. Joseph struck the rocky ground with his staff and out gushed a cooling spring. This is, they say, the Sisters' Fountain on the Glenthorne Estate which we pass on our walk.

Continuing on their way they came within sight of Glastonbury Tor rising from the marshes and made towards it. On a slope near the Tor they stopped to rest and Joseph knelt to pray, thrusting his staff into the ground. To the amazement of all it took root and blossomed. This miracle was taken as a sign from Heaven that they were meant to make this spot the site of the first Christian settlement in Britain. They approached the local King who granted them land where they set about building a church. This was the Old Church of wattle and daub over a frame of branches guarded so lovingly by the monks of Glastonbury until the disastrous fire of 1184 which destroyed it. The slope where Joseph's staff blossomed has been known for hundreds of years as Wearyall Hill, only ½-mile from the site of the Old Church in the Abbey grounds. There is the thorn tree planted to replace the Holy Thorn, cut down in Cromwell's time, which traditionally blossomed each Christmas. In the churchyard of St John's Church in the High Street there is also a fine thorn tree which blossoms in winter; the vicar sends a sprig each year to the Queen. Joseph buried the Holy Grail below the Tor for safe-keeping but we are told nowadays that it lies beneath the waters of Chalice Well (visited on our Glastonbury walk on p. 17), a place of pilgrimage in the Middle Ages.

Although no further convincing evidence has been found to support the story of Philip's mission to Gaul or Joseph's journey to Britain, the point is made by Geoffrey Ashe in his book *King Arthur's Avalon* that a visit to this country by a wealthy Jewish merchant, which conceivably Joseph may have been, is not entirely improbable. He could well have been one of the constant stream of travellers, military and civilian, whose business took them to the outlying parts of the Roman Empire. We cannot say of Joseph of Arimathea that he could not possibly have come here.

THE WALK:
A CIRCULAR ROUTE FROM COUNTY GATE DOWN TO GLENTHORNE BEACH, RETURNING VIA THE SISTERS' FOUNTAIN.
SHORT ALTERNATIVE FROM COUNTY GATE TO THE SISTERS' FOUNTAIN AND RETURN

MAP SQUARE G2
O.S. reference: 180/794486
Allow at least 2 hours for the circular route which is quite strenuous, dropping 1000 ft to the sea and back. Suitable for all ages. For the short walk to Sisters' Fountain and back allow 30 minutes at least.

County Gate is the Devon/Somerset border on the A39 between Minehead and Lynmouth: 12½ miles from Minehead and 5 miles from Lynmouth. There is a large car park, a site commanding magnificent views inland. From Easter to the end of September by the car park there is an Exmoor National Park Information Centre open from 10 am to 5 pm daily except Fridays. Maps and guides to the National Park are available, including a folder map of the Glenthorne Estate showing a number of walks.

Our Walk is based on one shown in the folder. The circular route provides not only some splendid views but is also of considerable natural history interest. The Walk to the Beach starts on the other side of the road opposite the County Gate car park and is signposted NATURE TRAIL.

The path descends at first along the eastern flank of the broad valley leading down to the sea, with view-points over the woodland on the other side of the valley and the sea. You may also be able to glimpse the large mansion, Glenthorne House, among the trees near the sea. Then through the woods past the Pinetum, a unique plantation of conifers of many species, mostly planted over 100 years ago and reaching to more than 100 ft in height. A further ½-mile down the path and you come to the Beach which consists of pebbles. Coal used to be landed here from South Wales and there are disused lime-kilns.

For the return route follow the signs HOME FARM and SISTERS' FOUNTAIN, the latter being the scene of Joseph of Arimathea's miracle and named after the four nieces of the founder of the Glenthorne Estate. The Cross at the Fountain was erected in the last century. From the Sisters' Fountain a steadily rising drive leads back to County Gate.

The short walk to the Sisters' Fountain starts at the same spot opposite County Gate as the Nature Trail mentioned above, but leads down to the left (westwards). The path is known as the Seven Thorns.

Glenthorne harbours many birds, particularly in the spring and autumn. Buzzards and kestrels are always to be seen. There are red deer in the woodland thickets but you are not likely to see them. However, you may find their tracks in the mud wallows near the stream you pass on the return section of the circular route.

There is a bus service on weekdays June–September between Minehead and Lynmouth calling at County Gate. In May the service operates on Mondays and Wednesdays only.

There are no refreshment facilities at County Gate.

NORTH CORNWALL

The Vicar of Morwenstow

'A Pair of Blue Eyes'
1. Thomas Hardy at St Juliot
2. Elfride and Henry on High Cliff

St Nectan's Kieve

The Coming of Arthur

The Mermaid's Revenge

The Giants of Trencrom

THE VICAR OF MORWENSTOW

The wild stretch of coast from Hartland Point to Bude is shared between Cornwall and Devon and just inside the Cornish boundary lies the large, lonely parish of Morwenstow. Anyone driving the 4 miles from the main A39 to Morwenstow will notice how few and far between are the farms and houses, and over the whole 7000 acres of the parish there are only 500 or so inhabitants. The isolation is emphasized when you approach Morwenstow by the coast path; for some miles either side you are walking along cliffs some 300–400 ft high, with sheer drops to the menacing rock formations below, against which the waves beat ceaselessly. In the 12 miles from Hartland Point to Bude there is only one harbour – Boscastle – where shipping can find any kind of shelter.

Morwenstow church and vicarage make an attractive sight from the cliff, in a setting of trees at the head of a steep bracken-covered combe running inland. Out of sight nearby are a large farm and, farther up the road, the Bush Inn and a few dwellings.

When Robert Hawker, the 31-year-old parson who in 1834 came with his wife to the parish, it seemed to be the end of the earth, but when he died 41 years later, still Vicar of Morwenstow, he had become a 'legend' and in that lonely scene made a name for himself as one of the 'personalities' of Victorian times. Son and grandson of Evangelical clergymen, Hawker followed in their footsteps and was ordained in 1831. After a rather boisterous boyhood he soon showed a streak of eccentricity or one might say an 'originality of approach' by marrying when he was 19 a lady of 40, the daughter of family friends. There have been allegations that he married for money but although she had a small income all the evidence shows that it was a love-match and when she died 40 years later he was heartbroken. In 1864 he was married again, to

Morwenstow Church. (*Edmund Swinglehurst*)

20-year-old Pauline Kuczynski who presented him with three daughters.

While at Oxford he had written poetry and as his time at Morwenstow progressed he drew much of his inspiration from the beauty of his surroundings. In a short time he seemed to have found his vocation in caring for his parishioners and in his writings. For the parish, he started by rebuilding a bridge on the road to Bude, a necessity in view of the very poor communications of the village. He then repaired the school and gave much time and attention to its affairs. The church had been much neglected and he put in hand restoration and repairs. For all these projects he raised funds through appeals, also using some of his own money. He then turned to his own needs and designed and built the vicarage, substantially the same as we see it now, and moved in with his wife from the cottage where they had lived since their arrival. The chimneys are said to be copies of the towers of the churches in which he had served before he came to Morwenstow. Over the front door he wrote:

A House, A Glebe, A Pound a Day,
A Pleasant Place to Watch and Pray.
Be true to Church – Be kind to poor,
O Minister, for ever more.

The contrast of his lot with that of his poor parishioners may not have occurred to him, but he seems to have been a good steward of his possessions. The vicarage may have been more grandiose than was needed but he explained that it would help to attract a good successor.

The favourite themes for Hawker's poetry came from Cornwall's past and her links with Irish, Welsh and Breton Christianity, but he is probably best known for his 'Song of the Western Men' written when he was only 22. The subject was probably the Bishop Trelawny, one of the seven bishops imprisoned in the Tower by James II. The refrain runs:

And shall Trelawny die?
Here's twenty thousand Cornish men
Will know the reason why!

Moved by the poverty of many of his flock he did what he could to help them. When he began the practice of distributing church collections to relieve the needy of the parish and, surprisingly, was criticized in many quarters, he defended his actions fiercely in letters to *The Times* and elsewhere. He tried to convey to those in better circumstances the condition of the rural poor, having to make a living on eight shillings a week, where a bad harvest could mean disaster. He is credited with first introducing the Harvest Festival service. This would have been quite natural as he once explained: an approaching harvest was a source of great anxiety, literally a matter of life or death, in that part of the world. At Christmastide he and his wife visited the parishioners with food and gifts and in times of illness he saw that the best attention available was given.

Hawker's eccentricities showed when he carried out his duties as a priest. A member of the High Church party of the Anglican Church he outdid his fellow clergy in his vestments and ritual. During services he would walk round the church, prostrating himself at intervals full length. In later years his outdoor dress consisted of a purple or claret-coloured coat, a blue fisherman's jersey and thigh-length seaboots. When riding he sported boots of bright red leather and curious hats. Medallions and other symbols of mystic significance were hung about his dress. When a cat came into the church during a service he told the congregation to leave it there.

One melancholy preoccupation which in the end began to affect Hawker's mind was with the all too frequent shipwrecks that took place within a stone's throw of his church. Piers Brendon in his book *Hawker of Morwenstow* has a whole chapter, based on his diaries and letters, spelling out the ghastly tragedies. Once a sailing vessel had been driven close

Morwenstow – *Caledonia* Figurehead. (*Edmund Swinglehurst*)

inshore by the terrible westerly gales there was little hope and it was only a matter of time before she would be torn to pieces on the rocks. At the news of a ship in distress Hawker and his men would clamber down to the beach with such tackle as they could lay their hands on and, often in darkness, do their best to help. Messengers would be sent to Bude and Clovelly where there were lifeboats but it was usually impossible for them to assist. The Morwenstow men could but watch helplessly and gather up the corpses or parts of corpses. A procession, led by Hawker intoning prayers, would pick its way up the cliff with the sad burden to await the inquest and burial. By 1870 he calculated that 40 victims of the sea had been buried in the churchyard. Survivors were very few but one such, from the wreck of the 200-ton *Caledonia* homeward-bound from Odessa in 1843, when he returned to his home in Jersey, used to send to Hawker, when he needed one, a cow of the best breed on the island. In the churchyard there is the figurehead of the *Caledonia*, remarkably well-preserved, placed over the grave of the captain and the crew, who all perished, save one.

Before Hawker came to Morwenstow, the inhabitants, in common with all their fellow Cornishmen living on the coast, used to regard a wreck as a gift from Heaven to help relieve their poverty. Some made a living from wrecks. Cruel Coppinger was one of these. A Danish seaman, survivor of a wreck of 1792, he carried on an organized trade in salvage from shipwrecks. He married a farmer's daughter and is said to have robbed her of her possessions and on occasions to have tied her to the bedpost. One day he vanished, presumably returning to Denmark with all the money and valuables he could find. At Morwenstow, Hawker's influence soon began to be felt and he noted with satisfaction after the wreck of the *Caledonia* that no part of its cargo had been stolen from the shore.

From the timbers of wrecks he built himself a small hut on the cliffside. There he used to sit and contemplate the scene before him and carry on with his writing. The hut is still there, having been taken over by the National Trust. Our recommended walk will show you how to get there.

Hawker died in 1875, having been received into the Catholic Church just before the end. With all his eccentricities and curious notions, his best deserved tribute came perhaps from one of his poorer parishioners: 'He was a good man.'

THE WALK:
TO THE CHURCH AND HAWKER'S HUT ON THE CLIFF AND BACK; WITH AN ALTERNATIVE CIRCULAR ROUTE FOR THE ENERGETIC

MAP SQUARE D3
O.S. reference: 190/209151
A flat even path to the Cliff and Hut. Allow 30 minutes each way. Alternative circular route, out to Hut, return via Henna Cliff. Allow 1½ hours. Hut walk suitable for well-supervised Under Eights. Circular walk not for young children.

For Morwenstow you turn off the A39 at Crimp or Wooley, 4–5 miles north of Kilkhampton. There is a green in front of the Bush Inn where you can park. A short way down the road towards the sea is the church and the vicarage. The vicarage is in private hands and is not open to visitors but you will want to see the church with its close associations with the Reverend Hawker. The building is of considerable interest. The unusual oval font is Saxon; Hawker attributed the founding of the church to Morwenna, one of the twenty-four sons and daughters of the Welsh King Breachan (after whom Brecon is named). There are traces of a wall-painting dating from about 1250 in the Sanctuary, which depicts Morwenna blessing a kneeling priest.

The Norman church was rebuilt in 1560. The three western arches of the nave are Norman and have been retained, the decorations on the second arch including curious heads: an owl, a hippopotamus and a man, which are repeated on the arch of the doorway of the church. The waggon-roof and the chancel screen are outstanding. There is a window dedicated to Hawker and other items to his memory. The booklet on sale in the church provides much fascinating detail.

The roadway to the church ends in a large gate and a kissing-gate stile with a National Trust sign MORWENSTOW VICARAGE CLIFF. Go through the stile and straight down the path which runs along the top of the southern slope of the valley. In a short while you come to the cliff and the coast path. Turn left (south) along the cliff path; a short way along on the right is a National Trust sign HAWKER'S HUT, which is a few feet below. The last occasion I was there, an elderly couple were sitting inside obviously enjoying the view as Hawker must have done on so many occasions. You return to the Bush Inn by the same route.

For something more strenuous, follow the path as outward to Hawker's Hut but on the return journey, instead of turning inland, continue northwards on the cliff path. Soon you will be descending a very steep and narrow path to the bottom of the valley (you cannot get down to the beach here). Over a footbridge and the slope climbs just as steeply upwards. At the top of the slope (the 400 ft summit of Henna Cliff is in front to your right), where the line of gorse ends, take the path on the right running inland along the field boundary. It later bears slightly left through a gap in the next field hedge and then continues along the south edge of the field where the gorse gives way to trees. You then come out on a sunken path in the trees leading on your right down to a footbridge over the stream and past the vicarage, to the road, not many yards from the Bush Inn.

There is a bus service on Wednesdays between Bude and Morwenstow (North Cornwall Cars Ltd) which gives visitors nearly four hours. Enquire about times in Bude.

In addition to the Bush Inn, lunch-time snacks and teas are served at Rectory Farm, near the church, from Easter to mid-October. They also provide accommodation.

'A PAIR OF BLUE EYES'

1. THOMAS HARDY AT ST JULIOT

Thomas Hardy is best known for his links with Dorset where he was born and grew up and which county forms the setting for most of his works. However, North Cornwall provides the scene for one of the most dramatic stages in his life and literary career.

In 1856 when aged 16 he was apprenticed to a Dorchester architect and for 14 years worked as an architect's assistant in London, Weymouth and Dorchester. In March 1870 he was sent down for a few days to St Juliot near Boscastle to report on the condition of the parish church which his employer had been commissioned to restore, and there at the rectory where he was staying he met Emma Gifford, the rector's sister-in-law. They were immediately attracted to each other. She was a bright, buxom, energetic young woman with blue eyes and a mass of fair hair and was quite a daring horsewoman. She was about Hardy's age and had been helping her sister in the rectory and the parish.

In August of the same year Hardy spent an idyllic three weeks' holiday at the rectory at the rector's invitation and the young pair spent many happy hours wandering over the beautiful countryside, discovering they had literary and other tastes in common. It was Hardy's first encounter with the awesome grandeur of the towering rocky cliff-girt coast of North Cornwall and in later years he was to recall in some of his best poetry the deep emotions of the courting of Emma in that incomparable setting. But it was also to provide the inspiration for the novel which was to put him firmly on the first rung of the ladder to ultimate literary fame. After having to pay a publisher to have his first novel published and his second, *Under the Greenwood Tree*, an apparent failure, he

St Juliot. *(Edmund Swinglehurst)*

was paid £200 for the story *A Pair of Blue Eyes*, which was ready by the following August.

In the tale a young architect, Stephen Smith, makes a professional visit to 'Endelstow' (St Juliot), a church near 'Castle Boterel' and falls in love with Elfride Swancourt, the rector's blue-eyed daughter, who ultimately agrees to elope with him to London. On arriving there, she decides not to marry him and returns home at once. She transfers her affections to a friend of Stephen's, an older man, Henry Knight, who has been encouraging Stephen to persevere with his writing. After hearing of Elfride's abortive elopement Henry breaks off the relationship. Elfride marries the local lord of the manor but the story has a sad ending.

Anyone who reads the novel and visits St Juliot will find scenes exactly as described: the delightful situation of the solitary church on a steep hillside with marvellous views over wooded valleys towards Lesnewth; the grey Victorian rectory standing four-square in its trees a few hundred yards away on the same slope and linked by field path with the church (the stone stile in the churchyard wall mentioned by Hardy is still there). One can easily imagine Hardy arriving by pony and trap from the station 16 miles away that March evening and being greeted by Emma – but what brings home more eloquently the atmosphere of that lyrical courtship is the beautiful lower valley of the Valency where the river runs from below St Juliot over its rocky bed through woods and past meadows with a footpath following its course for most of the way down to Boscastle. It was here that Hardy and Emma picnicked during one of their walks and as Emma was washing a wine glass in the stream it slipped, became wedged and somehow was lost. A sketch* of Hardy's executed on the spot portrays the scene which was movingly recalled after Emma's death forty years later, in the poem 'Under the Waterfall':

> By night, by day, when it shines or lours
> There lies intact the chalice of ours,
> And its presence adds to the rhyme of love
> Persistently sung by the fall above.
> No lip has touched it since his and mine
> In turns therefrom sipped lovers' wine.

A Pair of Blue Eyes was followed by *Far From the Madding Crowd* and other well-known Hardy works which established his reputation for ever. By 1874 he was able to give up his architect's career in order to devote all his time to writing. Emma and he were married in London in September of that year.

Many other local scenes in St Juliot are identifiable from the text of *A Pair of Blue Eyes*. The Legend on pp. 54–6 describes a cliff-top drama from the same book.

*The sketch can be seen at the Dorset County Museum, Dorchester and is reproduced in Robert Gittings' *Young Thomas Hardy*.

THE WALK:
BOSCASTLE TO ST JULIOT

MAP SQUARE D4
O.S. reference: 190/100913
Easy riverside footpath for 2 miles rising rather steeply for the last mile. Suitable for all the family but long for toddlers. Allow 1½ hours out, 1 hour home.

Boscastle is easily reached by car from the A39: by the B3266 from Camelford (if coming from the south); or by the B3263 from Tresparrett Posts (if coming from the north).

There are two large car parks in Boscastle: one (National Trust) on the harbour – where there is also a National Trust information bureau and shop – and one where the B3263 starts to climb out of the town. The path along the Valency valley starts just beyond the latter, by the side of the cottage Valency. The path crosses a meadow and then runs alongside the stream through woods until, after about a mile, you will reach Newmill with its few old cottages. At the fork of the path take the left one, through a white gate. The path begins to rise and you eventually come to a meadow with fine views of the upper valleys of the Valency and the other streams running into it. You will see three signposts: ST JULIOT to the left; ST JULIETTA straight on; and LESNEWTH to the right. If you wish to see the church first, carry straight on ('Julietta' should be 'Julitta' to whom St Juliot church is dedicated). Alternatively, if you wish to see the former St Juliot Rectory, take the path on the left which comes out into a lane past a large grey Victorian house. This is the rectory which played such a large part in Hardy's life and in which (as the 'Rectory of Endelstow') so many scenes took place in A Pair of Blue Eyes. *The house is now in private hands and cannot be visited. The lane joins a road; turn right and you will reach the church after a few moments. Much of the church was restored by Hardy's firm (including the rebuilding of the tower), the original church going back to the fifteenth century. Inside is a memorial to Hardy and one to Emma, the wording of which he wrote and included in his will. There are two ancient Crosses in the churchyard. The view from the churchyard over the stone stile is superb and must often have been enjoyed by Hardy and Emma. The return to Boscastle by the same path is quicker as it is downhill all the way. Hardy enthusiasts can amuse themselves by guessing which little waterfall on the Valency it was where the picnic glass was lost. A rewarding diversion can be made by crossing the footbridge a little over halfway down and following the path (that climbs out of the valley) to Peter Wood and Minster. This takes you to the old, secluded Minster church, formerly a priory, much restored from its thirteenth-century and Norman origins, with some sixteenth-century brasses. In spring there is a profusion of daffodils and bluebells. A road leads back to Boscastle, down the old main street with its delightful cottages. (Allow half an hour extra for this diversion.) Boscastle itself is full of interest, particularly the harbour, built by the famous Sir Richard Grenville in Elizabeth's reign. There is the famous blowhole through which the sea sprays out with great force. On the quay is the Witches' Museum with plenty of authentic grisly exhibits for those with strong stomachs.*

There is a bus service (Fry's) on most weekdays between Tintagel and Boscastle. Enquire locally for times.

You need to take all the food and drink you are likely to need as there are no shops at St Juliot.

2. ELFRIDE AND HENRY ON HIGH CLIFF

In Hardy's *A Pair of Blue Eyes* young Stephen Smith and his older friend, Henry Knight, are successively suitors of Elfride Swancourt of St Juliot. After Stephen's unsuccessful attempt at eloping with Elfride he takes a post in India for a year so that he can save enough money to marry Elfride on his return to England. His friend Henry, coincidentally and unknown to Stephen, has in the meantime met the Swancourts in London and, as a distant connection of theirs, is invited to St Juliot. He goes down there and falls in love with Elfride who is recovering from the elopement episode. Henry, however, does not give Elfride any idea of his infatuation although she has noticed a change in his attitude towards her and is not unmoved herself.

During Henry's visit, Elfride hears that Stephen has arrived back in England and is coming to St Juliot, making the journey from Bristol to Boscastle by steamer. She decides to watch for the steamer from the nearby High Cliff, one of the highest spots on the coast. On the cliff she runs into Henry who offers to accompany her although she does not tell him that she is expecting Stephen on the steamer. A strong wind is blowing as they stand on the cliff-top watching the steamer and Henry's hat is blown off. He tries to recover it, goes too near the edge, falls on the grassy slope and finds he cannot struggle back to the top. Elfride tries to reach him but also gets into difficulty and can only get back by using Henry's shoulder as a step. Henry, gradually slipping down the slope, manages to keep from falling over the edge to the sea 700 ft below by clutching a nearby bush, but his hold is made insecure by the rain which has started to fall. To Elfride, watching from the top, it seems certain he will fall to his death.

The Strangles. *(Edmund Swinglehurst)*

She suddenly disappears from Henry's view, returning after a few minutes with a bundle of linen – her underclothes, having replaced swiftly and demurely her outer dress which Henry, though in a desperate plight, notices clings rain-soaked to her youthful figure. Elfride sits on the grass and knots the undergarments together, producing a lifeline of sufficient length to lower to Henry and, tying one end round her own waist, is able to keep the line steady enough for Henry to haul himself the few feet to safety.

Henry regains his footing on the cliff and, panting, gazes at Elfride. The pair speechlessly fall into each other's arms and remain for some time overcome by relief – all the sweeter for being the first physical demonstration of the love that had been growing between them.

Hardy's 18-page description makes exciting reading although one wonders, with the changes in fashion in feminine underwear, what a modern Elfride would have done!

THE WALK:
TO STRANGLES BEACH OR
HIGH CLIFF

MAP SQUARE D4
O.S. reference: 190/134951
Wander at will through the level, wide gorse-clad cliff-top area with fine views, or down to Strangles Beach (15 minutes down; 30 minutes up) or to High Cliff (at least 30 minutes). Apart from High Cliff, and other areas near the cliff-edge, suitable for Under Eights if closely supervised.

The area can be reached in a few minutes from a lay-by on the secondary road which turns off the A39 or the B3263 westward towards the coast and Crackington Haven via Newton Farm (turning: about 1 mile before Marshgate if coming from north on A39; or 3 miles from Boscastle on B3263). The lay-by is about 2 miles along the secondary road. Opposite the lay-by is the National Trust sign for THE STRANGLES. The Trust owns a 2-mile stretch of magnificent cliff-top here. A short footpath leads to a crossing with the official Coast Path which southwards takes you past High Cliff or northwards to Cambeak, an impressive headland. A long, steep path leads down to The Strangles Beach (no swimming).

Of course, if you are a hardy walker you can reach The Strangles by the official Coast Path from Crackington Haven (about 1½ hours) or Boscastle (about 2½ hours).

For public transport, there is on certain days a bus (Tilleys Coaches) from Boscastle or Crackington Haven which takes you to the junction of the secondary road (ask for 'road to Newton Farm') leaving you a 1½–2-mile walk along the secondary road to The Strangles area.

There are no refreshment facilities on The Strangles although in high-summer season Trevigue Farm just north of the lay-by offers teas.

ST NECTAN'S KIEVE

St Brychan of Wales – he gave his name to Brecon – had twenty-four sons and daughters of whom St Nectan was the eldest son. All these sons and daughters became saints or martyrs and St Nectan was one of the most beloved saints of Cornwall. He built himself a cell and a small chapel at the head of a steep little wooded glen near Tintagel where a stream tumbles over a sparkling waterfall on its way down to the cliffs and the sea – 'kieve' means 'tub' or 'basin' in Cornish speech and can be translated here as 'pool'. The water ripples through a luxuriant growth of trees and woodland plants, the whole stretch in spring being loud with the songs of birds and carpeted with a profusion of wild flowers. Along the path through this little valley came the Cornish folk to hear God's word from the lips of the saint and to bring him the sick to heal.

In the tower of the chapel the saint placed a silver bell whose sweet notes could carry to the sea and beyond, cheering storm-bound seamen and their families ashore. When Nectan felt he was near to death he bade his followers take him to a rock overlooking the pool and to fetch him the silver bell. When they had given it into his hands he cast it into the pool. There, he said, it would remain for ever, safe from thieving and irreverent hands. Even though its sounds would no longer be heard, the people would know it was there under the water and its message would be the same as when he was alive.

After Nectan's death two mysterious sisters appeared and took over the cell and the chapel. When others approached they kept silence and everyone asked who they could be. Some said they could be two of his many sisters; others suggested that they were two holy women whom the saint entrusted with a special task on his behalf. Before long it was noticed that the sisters had gathered together all the vessels of silver and gold and the vestments from the chapel and placed them in a large chest. Then with their own hands they diverted the course of the little stream so that they were able to dig a large hole under the original course of the waterfall. In this hole they buried the chest and then restored the stream and the waterfall to its former bed thus locking away for ever the treasure of the saint.

The two sisters were seen over many years, always together, always silent, gathering plants and berries for food and tending the small garden they had laid out near the chapel. There came the day when those living nearby, not having seen the sisters in their normal surroundings, ventured to look into the chapel. There they saw one of the sisters sitting motionless beside the body of the other. They reverently enclosed the remains in a plain coffin and gave it burial. The lone sister was then often seen making her sad way through the glen and in her garden, but then she disappeared. A small child wandering one day plucked up courage and looked through the chapel window and there saw the sister sitting in her chair, with her hands stretched towards a handkerchief on the floor, as though she were unable to reach it. She, too, had died. Tradition has it that the two sisters are buried under a flat stone at the bottom of the glen.

The years went by and the now empty cell and chapel became a place of pilgrimage for all Cornwall. But certain miners, having heard of the legend of St Nectan's treasure beneath the waterfall, resolved to blast away the rock to see if they could find the chest. It was a relatively simple task to divert the stream and to blast the rock but as they were engaged in removing the debris they were stopped short by the clear sound of a bell and with terror-stricken senses they heard a voice saying, 'The child is not yet born who shall recover this treasure.' They ceased what they were doing at once and hurriedly directed the stream back to its former course. From that time none has dared disturb the peace of the Kieve.

St Nectan was buried at Hartland Abbey and became a much revered saint of pre-Conquest Britain. His venerated relics were treasured by many churches and a chronicle was written in the eleventh century listing all his miracles.

THE WALK:
TO THE WATERFALL IN
ST NECTAN'S GLEN.
OPTIONAL WALKS TO
ROCKY VALLEY AND THE
BEACH IN BOSSINEY
COVE

MAP SQUARE D5
O.S. reference: 190/076892
A pleasant 30-minute walk each way through woods. To Rocky Valley and back allow 30 minutes. Add on 30 minutes each way Rocky Valley to the beach. The first two walks are suitable for all ages. The cliff path from Rocky Valley to the beach is not suitable for Under Eights or the elderly (children could visit the beach from Bossiney village, as mentioned, but the path is steep for the elderly).

Two miles east of Tintagel on the B3263 Boscastle road lies the Rocky Valley Hotel. On the far side of the hotel, coming from Tintagel, by a phone box, there is a path with signs: PUBLIC FOOTPATH and TO ST PIRAN'S GARDEN. This is the most convenient path for the Waterfall. There is a field car park opposite the hotel; at times the small fee for visiting the Waterfall is collected here. The path soon forks by a small church; take the right-hand fork. After ½-mile of metalled drive, with one or two houses, the path slopes down through woods alongside a gurgling stream, eventually bringing you to a small house, the Hermitage, said to be built on the site of St Nectan's first cell. As mentioned, you pay a small fee to see the Waterfall. This is really spectacular. It is not its height which is so impressive – the drop is about 40 ft – but the rock formation over which the water passes. First, down to

Rocky Valley (*Edmund Swinglehurst*)

a small pool and then, from this pool, the water plunges through a large hole which it has worn through an arch of rock, into a larger pool, the Kieve itself, to continue as a stream over its rocky bed down to the sea at the end of Rocky Valley. Return by the same route.

There is an alternative return route from the Waterfall (taking about the same length of time) which will avoid road walking, if you wish to continue to Rocky Valley and the sea. From the Waterfall, follow the path along which you came until you reach a footbridge (the third on the way down) on your left. Cross this bridge over the stream and follow the path leading up from it through the woods to a kissing-gate entrance to a field. Do not continue towards the farm buildings on the right but, keeping half-left, climb the short, grassy field slope in front of you. From the top of this slope you will see on the field boundary opposite a gap in the wall with a PUBLIC FOOTPATH sign. Make for this and it will bring you on to a metalled road. Follow the road, past the building, Halgabron House, and after ¼-mile you will reach the main B3263 road.

For a visit to Rocky Valley (and, if you wish, the beach at Bossiney Cove) cross straight over the main road to the path signposted TO THE TROUT FARM (there is a small lay-by close at hand, on the main road). After a few yards you come to Trevillet Mill, an old mill that is being lovingly restored by its owners. Home-made teas and refreshments are served here in the season. Continue down the slope, the path following the stream in a narrow glen, beautifully wooded. About 200 yards down the path, on the right by a ruined mill, there are, on the rock, curious circular carvings about a foot across with 'maze-like' markings, believed to be of Bronze Age origin – 3000–4000 years old. You soon emerge on the Coast Path and a footbridge. You can probably find a spot on the slope above for a rest or picnic, enjoying the views of the splendid high cliffs.

To continue to the beach at Bossiney Cove you have first a steep climb from the footbridge and then, after a fine stretch of cliff path, a steep descent by a small stream to the beach, a favourite with the few, including children, who do not mind negotiating the long approach. For the return from the beach, take the 'sunken' path above the beach leading straight inland. After about 500 yards this comes out on the main B3263 in Bossiney village by the National Trust car park (a phone box is adjacent to the entrance).

If you have decided not to try Rocky Valley and the cliff path, you can reach the beach at Bossiney Cove from the National Trust car park mentioned above. The elderly might find the ascent from the beach arduous.

Bus services (Fry's) linking Tintagel and Boscastle and serving Trethevey and Bossiney run along the B3263 on weekdays. Enquire locally.

For refreshments there is a good pub, the Rocky Valley Hotel which has a garden, and the Trevillet Mill as mentioned.

THE COMING OF KING ARTHUR

Over most of Britain was waste, destruction and decay. Hordes of invaders; Celts from Ireland and Picts from Scotland, all of whom had never been subjected to Roman rule; fierce Germanic tribesmen from Denmark and Germany, descended on the Britons left defenceless by the departed Romans. Internally the petty regional kings spent more time squabbling among themselves than in trying to unite their peoples and encouraging them to resist the invaders. The pastures were unattended; the fields unsown; the woodlands overgrown and the animals scattered. The long-boats penetrated deep along the estuaries, the invaders putting whole villages to the sword, taking as slaves those whom they did not kill. In truth it was the Dark Age of Britain.

Leodogran who was, in name at least, King of Britain heard at his stronghold, Cameliard, stories of the feats of arms and noble character of Arthur who at Tintagel had been chosen king of the region. Dispirited by his lack of success against his country's raiders and weary of the ceaseless quarrels of his vassal kings he sent to Arthur and bade him bring his knights to help destroy the invaders and restore the land to its former prosperity.

So Arthur with his chosen knights rode over to Cameliard and, with Leodogran, came secretly upon the raiding bands and slew them to a man. Arthur then remained with the King for some weeks to help his people clear the woods and pastures and build their life anew.

King Leodogran had an only daughter, Guinevere, whose beauty cast radiance all around her like the sun. As Arthur was riding home past the King's castle Guinevere stood hidden watching him. Arthur, without raising his eyes, felt her gaze upon him, turning his heart to water and he returned to Tintagel, overcome with loneliness and desire for Guinevere.

In the days that followed, Arthur's feelings for Guinevere grew more and more intense and, calling Sir Bedivere, one of his companions lately raised to knighthood, he entrusted him with the mission to Leodogran to ask for Guinevere's hand for his master. When the King heard Arthur's request he was troubled in his mind and said to Bedivere, 'As you are well aware, I cannot give my daughter in marriage to any but a king's son. I have heard many tales of the birth of your liege lord: one says he was King Uther's heir; others that he was Prince Gorlois' son or is base-born. What is the truth?' Sir Bedivere answered, 'I do not know the truth but we believe he is the son of Uther, born before his time. Ygerne, wife of Gorlois, who held Tintagel, had daughters, one of whom is the good Queen Bellicent of Orkney, but no son. King Uther, who was also without an heir, desired Ygerne for wife and sought quarrel with Gorlois, slaying him. Taking over Tintagel he took Ygerne as wife. She bore him a son the night after Uther died. Merlin, Uther's wise magician, took the boy and entrusted his upbringing to a faithful courtier, to protect him from jealous lords.'

As Leodogran was turning over in his mind what Bedivere had told him, it so happened that Queen Bellicent of Orkney came to his court with her two sons, Gawain and Mordred. He told Bellicent of Arthur's wish and asked her what she knew of his birth.

Bellicent answered: 'Gorlois, Uther and Ygerne, my Mother, were dark of hair and eye, as I am, but Arthur is fairer than any Briton. I will tell you the truth, known only to me, to Merlin and Merlin's master, Bley, who before he died a few moons ago recounted to me the marvel.

'The night King Uther died Bley and Merlin, moved by some inner stirring, strode from Tintagel on to the beetling cliff. Thunder and lightning filled the dark skies. Suddenly, as they looked out to sea a long ship appeared, shimmering in a bright light which also bathed those who manned her. As she approached the cove below, Bley and Merlin descended with all speed to the beach but the ship vanished. As they watched, a huge wave, its crest blazing with a dazzling light, broke on the shore and, as it retreated, a small babe was left on the sand. As Merlin gently picked him up he cried, "Our King. An heir for Uther!" Then was he brought up by Anton, the faithful lord until, O King Leodogran, he was lately crowned. I was there at his crowning and saw, borne before him, the great sword, Excalibur, snatched from the lake by Arthur, as Merlin foretold and which will deliver us.'

The next day Leodogran sent Sir Bedivere back to Arthur, giving him the hand of Guinevere in marriage. In the spring Sir Lancelot, Arthur's bravest knight, brought Guinevere to Tintagel, and there in radiant white she and Arthur were wed while all stood and praised God.

THE WALK:
FROM TINTAGEL VILLAGE DOWN TO THE BEACH OF TINTAGEL HAVEN, THE CASTLE AND TINTAGEL CHURCH OF ST MATERIANA

MAP SQUARE D5
O.S. reference: 200/055886
Actual distance of walk, about 1½ miles – say, 1 hour, but the Castle site and the Church are well worth a visit. Suitable for Under Eights if closely supervised.

There are plenty of car parks in Tintagel. At the far (western) end of the main street the path down to the Castle is clearly signposted and you can also reach the beach this way by a short path near the hut where admission tickets to the Castle are sold. The beach is small and stony. On the left (west) side is a large cave which actually pierces the cliff through to the other side. At low tide you can enter the cave and penetrate quite a distance. This is the famous Merlin's Cave and traditionally is where the baby Arthur was washed ashore at the feet of Merlin and Brey.

Tintagel Castle has been in ruins for many years and the site now comes under the Department of the Environment who are in charge of preservation and excavations. The remains of the

Tintagel – Merlin's Cave. *(Edmund Swinglehurst)*

Castle: the Outer Ward on the mainland and the Inner Ward on the 'Island' (which was a real island until the causeway was built), in their magnificent setting, are full of interest, particularly if the excellent DOE booklet is followed. The Castle was built about 80 years after the Battle of Hastings by the Earl of Cornwall, illegitimate son of Henry I, who nearly became Holy Roman Emperor. Traces of his Great Hall can still be seen. Two hundred years later the Black Prince owned the Castle. To my mind, however, it is the faint traces of the little chapel on the Island which stir the imagination. In addition to a medieval chapel excavations have uncovered an early Celtic monastery. The chapel was dedicated to St Juliot (or Julitta), a missionary from South Wales who built his cell here about AD 500, shortly after the Romans left the country. Later there was a small monastery there and a settlement on the mainland nearby, by monks from Minster near Boscastle (see p. 53). The saint is perhaps one of the earliest of the devoted and beloved band of missionaries who served to keep alive the spirit of Christendom through the Dark Ages.

What of Arthur and Tintagel? The experts say there is no real evidence of a connection. But there seems to be a general agreement that some leader arose, probably in the south-west, who united and inspired the Britons to defy successfully for some years the Nordic and other invaders. A very fair picture of the Arthurian question is given on pp. 10–13 of the DOE booklet. Whatever the answer may be to the mystery, the Island of Tintagel and its inhabitants of 1500 years ago seem to embody an heroic chapter in our history and a gleam of Christian faith in the darkness.

After the Castle and the beach, if you wish to visit the church follow the sign TO THE CHURCH a short way back up the path to Tintagel. This path will lead you in a few minutes to the top of the cliff and the Church of St Materiana, the church of Tintagel, standing alone on the cliff. This is a most interesting building which has been looked after with great care and has features from Norman times through to the fifteenth century. There is a fifteenth-century brass and even an inscribed stone of Roman origin, said to be dedicated to the Emperor Licinius, put to death by Constantine in AD 324 who succeeded him. It was Constantine who decreed Christianity to be the religion of the Empire.

There is a roadway leading back to Tintagel. To say Tintagel village is a disappointment is an understatement. Redeeming features are the Old Post Office in the main street – an example of a small fifteenth-century manor-house now owned by the National Trust, and the Hall of Chivalry, in the same street, with many exhibits illustrating the legend of Arthur.

THE MERMAID'S REVENGE

In the village of Perranzabuloe which lies a short distance inland from the well-known town of Perranporth (although at the time of our story this resort was very much smaller than it is today) lived a certain family: Penna, the husband, who worked on a neighbouring farm, Honour, his wife, and their daughter, Selina. It is not an uncommon occurrence in most communities when, for some reason or other, a person or a family, although playing a full part in the community, stands a little apart from the rest and this was the case with Penna and his small household. Penna himself was not local born but came from near Marazion on the south Cornish coast; he has been engaged by the Squire of Perranzabuloe who had heard of his abilities in farm management and of his strength of character. He had been entrusted with the running of a small outlying farm under the general supervision of the Squire's agent, Tom Chenalls, and had benefited from the Squire's confidence. On coming to the village he had met Honour and had been at once attracted by her good looks and serene manner. Before many months they were married and settled down in a cottage which soon stood out among the others that were clustered around them for the brightness of its whitewashed walls, the neatness of its flower beds and a general air of being well looked after.

There was one cloud which threatened from time to time to darken their happiness. Tom Chenalls, for some time – long before Penna's arrival in the village – had admired Honour but she would have nothing to do with him. Tom, although he made a competent agent of the Squire's large estate, was sly and secretive and she felt he could not be trusted. His attentions to Honour were beginning to be most irksome when Penna arrived on the scene and, much to her relief, began courting and eventually married her. Unfortunately Tom could not forget how he had been slighted and Honour's

Perranzabuloe. *(Edmund Swinglehurst)*

preference for one whom he considered much inferior to himself in every way. His jealousy took the form of making Penna's life as difficult as he could – fault-finding and constantly picking a quarrel. Penna determined not to be provoked and this upset Honour who felt he should stand up to Tom and if necessary complain to the Squire.

The one unclouded joy of their lives was their daughter, Selina. At the time of our tale she was 18 and of an unusual beauty. Although her parents were dark-haired and brown-eyed her eyes were as blue as the sea on a cloudless day and her hair fair as the golden sand. In many ways she seemed to live in a world of her own, often sitting on the cliff above Perranporth gazing for hours out to sea, which from her earliest years seem to have had a fascination for her. As soon as she could walk her parents took her with them on the shore; they would take her into the water and teach her to swim but were startled on one occasion when she evaded them and dashed into the waves, riding the crests with every confidence and swimming and diving like a young dolphin. As she grew older she spent more and more time in the sea, staying in the water for an hour at a time and showing no fear even when the wind whipped the waves to a great height.

The Squire's nephew, Richard Trelawney, a young man who had been wounded in one of the Indian campaigns, came to Perranzabuloe to regain his health. He soon noticed Selina and fell deeply in love with her. He spent much of his time with Tom Chenalls who was able to introduce him to the best places for shooting and other field sports. Noticing Richard's infatuation Chenalls, although he knew Selina was one of the most virtuous girls in the neighbourhood, persuaded Richard otherwise, convincing him that she should be easy prey. The lovers began to meet secretly, spending long hours in the Perran sandhills and in the fields. Selina in her impressionable innocence believed her lover when he told her that he was only waiting to pick up again the threads of his life that had been broken by his wounds for them to be married.

The poor girl was shattered when Richard went back to London without telling her or leaving a message. Her parents became more and more worried as they saw the fit of melancholy which seemed to have gripped her and when she told them she was pregnant they were overcome by grief, but far from condemning her they could not do enough to cheer her and help her through her difficult time. After a few months she gave birth to a daughter who died within two days. The baby's death was followed by that of Selina herself.

Everything began to go wrong for Tom Chenalls. In the management of the Squire's estates his judgement began to falter. He chose the wrong time to sow the seed, causing the crops to fail, and he quarrelled with the workers who began to query his orders. He seemed to go to pieces. He took to drinking heavily and became incapable of carrying out his duties, leaving the Squire with no option but to dismiss him. He spent his days in his cottage on the cliff drinking and trying in his sober intervals to tend his small plot.

Richard Trelawney was seen again in the village. He and Tom spent most of their time together and many wild parties took place in the cottage on the cliffs. One night as Richard was staggering home, he missed the path although it was bright moonlight and found himself by the rocks fringing the small bay. He was startled to hear the most beautiful singing coming from the rocks. As though attracted by a magnet he stumbled his way to where the voice seemed to come from and was stopped short on seeing a woman's figure. She made the loveliest sight imaginable: her white skin shone in the moonlight and her long hair was like a golden diadem crowning an exquisite face. Suddenly she saw him and her song stopped abruptly. She stretched out her arms towards him; he fell into them with a cry: 'Selina! Selina!' It was indeed she, somehow transformed into an ethereal being of the sea. They remained locked in each other's arms. Her embrace was fierce and cold. 'I have you now for ever; bring me back the one who is dead!' She planted a kiss on his lips and on his forehead. They were icy. Suddenly he felt the water lapping around his ankles; the tide was coming in fast but her embrace held him. He struggled but it was of no use. The water came higher and higher until they floated off on a huge wave. He could not breathe; he was choking; as his senses left him all he could hear was her voice in his ear: 'You must come with me now, and for ever!'

THE WALK:
A CIRCULAR WALK FROM PERRANPORTH ALONG THE COAST PATH TO CLIGGA HEAD, RETURNING BY PATH THROUGH FIELDS

MAP SQUARE B6
O.S. reference: 204/757543
A 1½–2-hour walk not really suitable for Under Eights. They will be very happy on the sands of Perranporth.

The Walk starts at the large car park on the front in Perranporth, always extremely busy in the season – but you will be almost alone on the Coast Path. Take the road at the car-park entrance; this climbs quite steeply towards the cliff-top. You come to an open grassy space (a few cars can park here). Keep straight on making for the roadway behind the large Droskyn Castle Hotel. At the end is the entrance to an Admiralty establishment. On the left of the gate there is a PUBLIC FOOTPATH sign to St Agnes. Follow the path indicated and you will emerge on the 250-ft high cliff with the path winding its way, clinging to the indentations in the coast, with stupendous views. You will be able to imagine Selina sitting by the path gazing at the mass of water beneath, rising and falling, its breakers dashing themselves against the rocks so many feet below.

After ¾-hour to 1 hour walking on the path you approach a promontory, Cligga Head, where a large outcrop of granite, made bare by quarrying, seems to block the way, but the path picks its way past the protruding boulders with their remarkable strata formation. There are many signs of abandoned mines in the area including 'adits' or artificial channels for the water that was used. Granite is still quarried here and at the quarry site you turn inland, following the main track made by the lorries that cart away the rock. When you top the small rise you will see in front of you buildings and the end of the former war-time airfield, now used extensively at weekends by flying and glider clubs. The lorry track will bring you out on the road, passing on your left the largest airfield building. Facing you, on the opposite side of the road you should spot the start of a path with a PUBLIC FOOTPATH sign and a stile.

Cross the stile and follow a pleasant field path sloping downwards, with more stiles. When you reach a farm track you will see on your left in a hedge on the other side of the track another stone stile. Over this and continue across the field towards the cottage ahead of you. The path runs alongside the cottage to join a narrow road with many charming houses. Keep to the road, down the slope; turn left on reaching a wider road bordering a small stream. This will bring you soon to the gardens in the centre of Perranporth and to your car park.

Perranzabuloe ('sands of Piran' in Cornish) is now only a small hamlet, consisting of a church, a farm and a few houses on the A3075 on the outskirts of Perranporth. The church is the parish church of Perranporth. Perhaps the old farm nearby is the one that belonged to Squire Trelawney.

Perranporth is linked by bus with Newquay and many other centres in the area.

THE GIANTS OF TRENCROM

Most countries have their Giants. The Greeks had the Cyclops; in the Bible there is Goliath and throughout Europe the Giants Grim and Blunderbore have many stories told about them. Legends of whole races of giants are not, after all, too difficult to understand: even in the present day you have warrior races in eastern Africa who are exceptionally tall: how gigantic they must seem to the pigmies of equatorial Africa!

The poet John Milton, when he wrote an early history of Britain, tells how Trojan heroes Brutus and Corineus, with their band of warriors, after searching the seas for a new land in which to settle, landed on an inlet on the south coast of Britain, near where Plymouth now stands, and were confronted by a host of giant warriors who were only subdued after a fierce battle. Their leader, the giant Gogmagog, survived and challenged the Trojans to personal combat. Corineus accepted and a fierce battle took place. At one point the giant managed to grapple Corineus in a bear-like hug, cracking four of his ribs, but the Trojan was able to release himself and lifting Gogmagog off the ground hurled him into the sea. It is curious that on the other side of the country the tale of Gogmagog transformed him into the two giants, Gog and Magog, who are said to be the founders of the City of London; their gigantic carved figures decorate the sedate Guildhall of the City and look down on its prestigious proceedings.

Some members of the giant race, said to have fought against the Trojan invaders, could have come from their stronghold on the top of the 400-ft Trencrom Hill between Hayle and St Ives. Here, a regular-shaped gorse-and-heather-covered hill which stands out sharply against the surrounding scene is crowned on its summit by a mass of huge granite boulders scattered as though they had been hurled through the surface by some gigantic subterranean explosion.

It was here that the Giants of Trencrom had their home and it was they who manhandled some of the masses of granite and fashioned them into rough ramparts whose traces can today be discovered by the visitor. Archaeologists confirm that the huge rocks making up these defences must have been moved by human hand, and who else could have done this but Giants? The experts date the hill fort at the second century BC; and outlines of hut dwellings can be discerned on the surface.

The Giants of Trencrom were great friends of the Giants of St Michael's Mount which stands out dramatically 4 miles to the south. There was nothing they liked better than a game of skittles. The 'pins' – large rocks lying about the Hill – were set up, first on the Mount, and the Trencrom Giants would throw their 'skittle balls' – rocks roughly shaped like globes or cheeses – at the skittles 4 miles away. Then it would be Trencrom's turn to put up the skittles and the others to throw and see how many they could knock down. This was great fun for all – the only trouble was the terrible panic which was caused by the game among everyone living within 20 miles of the two places. The landing of each skittle ball made the earth shake as though in an earthquake and the raucous shouts of the Giants calling out the scores sounded like fearful claps of thunder.

Another story is told of the time when the chief of the Giants on St Michael's Mount wanted to borrow a sledge-hammer from his friend on Trencrom. 'Coming over!' shouted the friend as with a mighty throw he sent his huge hammer whistling through the air. The wife of the Giant on the Mount, hearing some commotion, looked out of the window to see what was happening and caught the hammer full on the head, breaking her skull and sending her body flying into the sea. The spot where she landed was where the little Chapel Rock now stands jutting out of the sea between the Mount and the shore just west of the causeway.

Some, however, say that the Chapel Rock, reputedly composed of greenstone unlike the Mount which is of granite, has another origin. The first Giant of St Michael's Mount was, with his wife, building the Mount with boulders of granite from the mainland so he could have a stronghold free from interference. One day, when they had nearly finished their mammoth task, the wife, tired from having to bring the heavy granite from the shore, and forced to go further inland each time to find suitable boulders, spotted on the beach a piece of greenstone rock of suitable size. She picked this up and was secretly trying to place it among the granite forming the walls when her Giant husband saw what was happening and with a mighty roar of rage gave her a terrible blow, knocking her, lifeless, into the sea. Her body, they say, lies under the Chapel Rock with the piece of greenstone rock on top of her as a memorial.

I really don't know which story to believe. I will leave you to make your choice.

THE WALK:
TO THE TOP OF
TRENCROM HILL

MAP INSET
O.S. reference: 203/518359
A short walk from the road of 15 to 20 minutes' duration.
Suitable for all.

Trencrom Hill lies on a secondary road branching from the A3074 Hayle–St Ives road. After leaving the A30 and turning up the A3074 towards St Ives you come almost immediately to a roundabout. Turn right to the second roundabout then follow the left-hand (westward) road signposted NANCLEDRA. When the road forks (at Lelant Downs) bear left (CRIPPLESEASE). You soon come across the slopes of Trencrom ¾-mile from the fork; just past the Gonew View Caravan Site there is a small car park on the right, from where there is a clear path leading to the top of the hill.

Alternatively, from Lelant Downs you can take the narrow road signposted TRENCROM (which is actually a farm). After a few minutes you will see a National Trust sign TRENCROM HILL on the left. There is a small lay-by for one or two vehicles or you might find space on the verge. From the sign there is a footpath to the top. The first route given is really the best for parking.

Once you arrive at the rock-covered summit you have a marvellous view of the countryside – 'from sea to sea': St Ives Bay in the north and, to the south, Mounts Bay. The 2½-mile-long sands of Hayle Beach stretch to the north, with Godrevy Point and the lighthouse on Godrevy Island at the far extremity of the beach. Turning to the south you can take in the magnificent 200-ft pile of St Michael's Mount with its ancient castle and church.

After enjoying the view you can perhaps amuse yourself by looking for traces of the Trencrom Hill 'fort': the rough ramparts with the gaps between the huge rock walls filled in with blocks of squared masonry and rubble and, within the ramparts, foundations of circular hut-dwellings.

The maze of paths and the rocks can make a fine playground for the children as long as you remain on the top to keep them in view.

The nearest bus-stop to Trencrom Hill is Cripplesease (1½ miles) on the Penzance–St Ives Western National bus route 516.

There are no refreshment facilities at the Hill.

LAND'S END

Cherry and the Fairy Widower
The Devils of Carn Kenidjack
Madgy Figgy's Chair
The Logan Rock
The Spectre Bridegroom
Duffy and the Devil

CHERRY AND THE FAIRY WIDOWER

Everyone who visits Cornwall has heard of the fairies known as 'Piskies'. Pictures of Piskies, Piskie dolls, Piskie postcards – the shops are full of them. But what is not generally known, is that there are at least five kinds of Cornish fairy-folk. The Piskie is a mischievous sprite – like Puck in *A Midsummer Night's Dream* – who loves playing harmless tricks on innocent mortals. There are the Spriggans who live in the caves and the cairns, and in the old prehistoric stone tombs which are dotted over the landscape, particularly in the Land's End area. If the farmer's cows are taken ill or the milkmaid's pail mysteriously keels over and spills all the milk, the Spriggans are blamed – they do more damage than Piskies ever would. Then there are the Bockles who live deep in the mines. They were heard sometimes knocking to give the miners warning of cracks in the mine gallery, telling them to get out quickly. Also, the household fairies, the Browneys, who are wholly good and do what they can for the family they live with, especially helpful when the bees are swarming. Most numerous of all the fairies are, however, the 'Little Folk'. These are fairy spirits of those who lived in Cornwall thousands of years ago. Their kings, queens and leaders have the power to change themselves into human shape when necessary and from time to time the Cornish people come into contact with them.

One such was Cherry. Cherry was a 16-year-old Cornish girl who lived with her parents and a host of brothers and sisters in a small cottage on top of the cliffs that tower over Treen Cove a mile or two from Zennor. They were a poor family but on the whole were contented enough. Their small plot of land produced root crops and vegetables and there were the fish and shell-fish from the sea and the pig or two they kept. One who was not so contented was Cherry, a well-built healthy girl with a spirited look in her eye which

Zennor. *(Edmund Swinglehurst)*

was indicative of an independent, adventurous nature. One thing that particularly irked her was that her parents could never afford to buy her a dress to go to the Morvah Fair. Each year the girls from nearby farms and villages would come past, riding pillion on their boyfriend's horse – sometimes even as many as three on one horse – urging her to jump up and come with them, but she was never able to do so. The problem was: where could she get the money? Her parents wanted her to go to the nearby village of Towednack and find a job with a family there, but this had little attraction as she knew the money would be very little and the Towednack people were not lively enough for her.

In the end she made up her mind to leave home and find a place where she could earn more and buy as many pretty dresses as she wished. Vainly her parents tried to dissuade her, pointing out all the pitfalls and dangers of going off like this on her own, but her mind was made up. So one hot summer's day she set off over the moor in a direction she thought vaguely would lead her to Penzance, which was to her an El Dorado. In those days, a long time ago, there were very few proper roads, only tracks, and the one she had taken climbed higher and higher and she became more and more tired and dispirited. She came to where two tracks crossed on the top of what is known as Lady Downs; here she sat on a stone and burst into tears, overwhelmed by homesickness.

After a few moments she dried her tears and decided to make her way back home and was just getting up from the stone when to her astonishment – she hadn't heard any footsteps – she saw in front of her a splendidly dressed gentleman in a flowered waistcoat, shining boots and with an elegant cane. He spoke to her in a most pleasant voice and asked who she was and what she was doing there. Cherry told him her name and why she was such a long way from home. 'Well, this is a very lucky occurrence,' said the gentleman. 'As it happens, I am a widower and I am looking for someone to keep house for me and to take charge of my little boy. You look a nice, intelligent girl. Would you like to come to my house and make it your home? I will guarantee you will like it.' Cherry did not need long to make up her mind and said eagerly, 'Yes, sir, I would love to come.'

So the gentleman strode down the hill with Cherry walking beside him. On and on they walked and Cherry wondered where they were going. After what seemed like many miles the way seemed to grow darker and they entered a grove of trees. A wide bubbling stream crossed their path and the gentleman took Cherry in his arms and carried her across. It was almost pitch dark when suddenly they came to a garden gate. They went through and all was light again. There was a beautiful garden, with beds of flowers of every possible colour and scent, and a path leading to a little house, its paint and windows shining in the sun. A little boy about 3 years old came running to them and the gentleman took him into his arms saying to Cherry, 'This is my son who you will be looking after.' The child, who had a rather grown-up look to his face, regarded Cherry with a serious expression, but before she could say anything, an ugly bent old lady came grumbling out of the house and dragged the boy back through the door. 'That is Aunt Prudence,' explained the gentleman. 'She is my wife's grandmother but she will go as soon as you have learned your duties.'

Aunt Prudence laid a nice meal for Cherry and afterwards took her up to her room at the top of the house where she would sleep, with the child in the same room. She was told she must close her eyes as soon as she was in bed and keep them closed even if she was not asleep. At dawn she was to get up and take the boy down to the pool in the garden which was fed by a sparkling spring gushing out of the rock. There she was to give him a good wash every morning. Beside the pool was a crystal box containing an ointment; she was to smear this ointment on the child's eyelids but on no account was she to put any of it on her own. After that, she was to milk the beautiful gentle cow that was tethered at the bottom of the garden and give the milk to the child for his breakfast. The rest of the day she could do the chores and help the master tend the garden with its plentiful vegetables, fruit and flowers.

Cherry was told she must keep to the kitchen and her bedroom and must not try to enter the other rooms, but she was dying to see what was in them. She was surprised one day when the old woman, who was obviously jealous of her, said she would show her the rest of the house. They passed down a long dark passage and then Cherry was told to take off her shoes. They then entered a large room with a floor like glass. It was filled, on shelves and on the floor, with stone figures of people, many of whom were without limbs or heads. Cherry was scared to death for she remembered having been told of people who had been turned to stone by the fairies. She wanted to rush out but Aunt Prudence made her go on until they stood before a large black coffin-like box. 'Polish this,' shouted Prudence. 'Rub it. Harder! Harder!' By this time Cherry was terrified and tried to escape, pulling over the coffin which fell with a crash. Disturbed by the noise, the master came hurrying in and drove the old lady away, carrying Cherry to the kitchen. After that Cherry did not see Aunt Prudence again.

The days passed very pleasantly but Cherry became determined to know why the child had to have the ointment on his eyes and one day she smeared some on her own eyelids. Immediately her eyes began to burn most painfully and she rushed to the pool to bathe them and there, to her amazement, she saw in the depth of the water, dozens of tiny people, dressed very elegantly, playing and dancing with her master in their midst, obviously enjoying himself thoroughly. As she looked round the garden she saw that in all the trees and on the grass lawns the little people were dancing, running and talking among themselves and swinging on the tree branches. Her master returned in the evening in his human form but Cherry said nothing to him about what had happened. After supper he went into the secret room and Cherry could not resist looking through the keyhole. There, to her annoyance, her master was dancing with a beautiful little princess who let him kiss her repeatedly.

The next day Cherry was helping her master gather fruit in the garden and, as was customary, when he went to give her a kiss as thanks for her help she slapped his face, saying, 'Don't kiss me! Go and kiss your fairy lady-love!' 'Ah!' said the gentleman. 'You have disobeyed me and have stolen the ointment. You must go and Aunt Prudence must come back to look after the boy.'

That very night, taking Cherry's bundle and a lantern, they set off through the dark grove and at daylight found themselves on the moor where they first met. Here her master set her on her way. 'You can never return to my house,' he said, 'but if you come up here when the moon is full, you may see me again.' Sadly Cherry went home and related everything that had happened to her, but even though she climbed up to Lady Downs many times at the full moon she never saw the fairy widower again.

THE WALKS:
TWO WALKS TO THE ANCIENT SITES:
1 CHUN CASTLE AND CHUN QUOIT
2 MEN-AN-TOL AND MEN SCRYFA

MAP SQUARE A7 (Inset)
O.S. reference:
Walk 1 203/409336
Walk 2 203/419344
The starting points of both Walks are close together. They are suitable for all ages. Allow ½ hour for Walk 1. Allow 1 hour for Walk 2.

These two Walks are along pleasant paths running over bare 700-ft-high moorland as was crossed by Cherry that summer's day. It is dotted with prehistoric sites – chamber tombs, hill-forts, stone circles, and so on – all likely to give rise to stories of the supernatural in the minds of the later inhabitants. They are based on an itinerary suggested to visitors to the Wayside Museum at Zennor, should they wish to see the most important archaeological remains in the area. The Wayside Museum, associated with the Cornwall Archaeological Society, with its unique collection illustrating Cornish life since earliest times should not be missed. Open daily from Whitsun to the end of September, entrance is free. When in Zennor make sure to visit the church. In a side-chapel there is a pew-end with a carving of the Mermaid of Zennor, which could go back to the fourteenth century. The legend of the Mermaid tells how she fell in love with the squire's son who had a beautiful voice. She lured him into the sea at Pendour Cove and he was never seen again although his voice is sometimes heard, they say, singing to his mermaid bride. There are two very early Cornish crosses in the churchyard.

Chun Castle and Chun Quoit are reached by a narrow turning off the Penzance–Madron–Morvah road (Morvah lies on the B3306 St Ives–Zennor–St Just coast road). About 4 miles from Penzance or 1½ miles from Morvah is Bosullow Common with its isolated schoolhouse. The narrow turning is signposted TO CHUN CASTLE on the south side by the schoolhouse. Cars

The Men-an-Tol. (*West Country Tourist Board*)

are parked for a small fee by the farmhouse at the end of the lane. The path to Chun Castle is indicated by markers.

Chun Castle is one of the best-preserved Iron Age hill-forts in Cornwall and dates from about 200 BC. There are remains of two high stone ramparts with inner and outer defensive ditches. The entrance is S-shaped for additional security. The fort was used again during the Dark Ages (sixth century). There is a well inside. About 100 yards or so to the west of the Castle is the chamber tomb of Chun Quoit, one of the few where the stones have not been dislodged, consisting of huge granite slabs for the support and roof. It could have been constructed as long as 4000 years ago. Such tombs were originally covered by earth. Human remains have been found.

Back to the schoolhouse, and on the opposite side of the road will be seen a path with a sign indicating the route to the MEN-AN-TOL and the MEN SCRYFA. You can park on the verge. About ½-mile up this path from the road you pass an empty farmhouse on your left. A few yards further on, on your right, is a sign to the MEN-AN-TOL ('holed stone'). This upright stone slab with a large hole, flanked by two stone pillars, is of unknown

Lanyon Quoit. (*West Country Tourist Board*)

function or origin. The hole is large enough for a reasonably sized adult to pass through – we are told children were passed through as a cure for rickets.

Continue for a further 600 yards along the main path and ahead of you to your left will be seen a stone pillar in a field. A path leads up to the Men Scryfa ('written stone'). This bears an inscription in Latin to 'Rialobran', who may have been a local chief of the fifth or sixth century, after the departure of the Romans.

Back on the road; if you wish to see another chamber tomb, 1 mile down, towards Penzance, in a field on the left near the road, is Lanyon Quoit (National Trust).

There is an infrequent bus service to Bosullow Common from Penzance and St Just. There is also a summer service St Ives–Zennor–Morvah–Land's End. Bosullow is a 1½-mile walk from Morvah.

There are no refreshment facilities at any of the sites mentioned. The Tinners Arms pub in Zennor can be recommended.

THE DEVILS OF CARN KENIDJACK

The high rock-strewn and wind-swept moor just north-east of the town of St Just and the area between the moor and the sea contain the essence of the true Celtic part of Cornwall. On this lonely stretch, shown on the map as Carnyorth and Truthwall Commons, within the compass of 1 mile are to be found the remains of three ancient stone circles and four tumuli or other form of prehistoric burial chamber, all contributing to a strong sense of the distant past. Between the moor and the sea are the more recent sites of dozens of abandoned tin mines, each one a witness of despair and abandoned hopes.

It is not unnatural, therefore, that this sombre landscape has been the scene of many a legend of the supernatural and the strangest of these has the setting of Carn Kenidjack, the heap of rocks on the highest point of the moors.

Two miners from one of the mines were walking home on a Saturday night. In the middle of the last century, each mine employed many hands and were in full production of the precious tin ore. After a day of the most exacting physical labour they had stopped to have a drink at the old Queen's Arms at Botallack before they started to cross the moor on their way home. They were startled to hear the thud of horses' hooves behind them and turned to see one of the lean half-wild ponies that often grazed there, with a rider in a black coat and hood, making for them at a furious pace. They hailed the unknown and asked where he was bound for. 'The wrestling on the Carn,' was the answer. 'Why don't you come and see for yourselves?' And horse and horseman dashed up the slope, the hooves of the horse seeming hardly to touch the ground. At the same time the two friends noticed a faint glow above them round the top of the Carn with shadowy figures flitting in and out.

The strong south-west wind blowing hard over the moor

produced the queer moaning sound which had given the name of 'hooting carn' to Kenidjack and brought a sinister atmosphere to the whole scene as they followed the horseman up the slope. When they reached the Carn they were astonished to see a large group of figures, all of similar appearance, squatting round a flat expanse just below the Carn which was obviously the wrestling ring. Each of the figures was dressed in black, had a long hooked nose and eyes that flashed like coals of fire. There was a loud and excited chattering which stopped abruptly when our horseman walked into the ring. From the deferential manner of those who moved to let him pass it was evident he was one in authority. He was in fact Old Nick himself. He was followed by another in black who was of slighter build. They took off their black cloaks and shirts and were bare to the waist. Their chests were broad and their waists narrow. The powerful muscles were revealed and despite the small difference in physique of the second entrant a close match was obviously to follow.

After circling, watching each other's slightest movement, the two contestants moved like lightning into a fierce grapple with their arms locked, each making violent efforts to get a neck-hold or a rib-breaking hold round the waist. They circled round the ring, to demon-like cheers and screams from the onlookers, their skins shining with sweat and uttering deep gasps as they filled their lungs, straining for a decisive hold. Suddenly Old Nick dropped his arms and grasped his opponent round the waist and, with a loud hiss through clenched teeth, lifted him from the ground and threw him high in the air. He hit the ground with a thud which sent a tremor through the earth and lay with limbs that twitched for a few moments and then were still.

The onlookers surged round the winner shouting, cheering and screaming, leaving the other lying still on the ground. Our two miner friends ran over to his side and one gently raised his head. But there was no doubt, he was dead. Good

Christians that they were, the two friends murmured a prayer and reverently crossed themselves. Instantly there was a vivid streak of lightning and a terrifying clap of thunder; a cloud of vapour hid the ring and those who crowded round it who could be heard screaming shrilly. The vapour cleared and the scene was as empty as a desert. The hordes of evil had been scattered.

Dazed and with unsteady step, the two friends walked away slowly down the slope towards their homes.

THE WALK:
FROM WHEAL BAL TO
CARN KENIDJACK

MAP INSET
O.S. reference: 203/382335
Short level walk, about 20 minutes, by path across heathland. Suitable for all ages.

The start of the Walk is Wheal Bal Hill, a short rise on the B3318 about ½-mile from where it turns off at Trewellard, 1½ miles north of St Just on the B3306 St Just–St Ives road. There is no proper parking space but you could probably park at the start of one of the tracks that lead over the heath. The track on which you commence the walk starts alongside the one house which is situated on the south side of the road on Wheal Bal Hill (the name, incidentally, probably refers to a disused mine nearby; 'wheal' is Cornish for 'mine'). The track becomes a footpath over the heath in the direction of Carn Kenidjack, a pile of large rocks on an eminence which you should be able to see to the left in front of you. The attraction of the open rocky heathland dominated by the Carn, 600 ft above sea level, may not be clearly apparent but when you arrive there is a fine view over the surrounding countryside which must have been the home of, or of religious significance to, the earliest inhabitants of the peninsula 4000 or more years ago. The children can climb on the rocks and run about over the heath – they will always be in view in that flat expanse. You will realize what a splendid spot the Devils chose for their wrestling match!

The Ordnance Survey map shows the area dotted with tumuli (burial mounds), stone circles, etc., but most of these are not easily detected. The best preserved, however, is probably the Tregeseal stone circle, about 3000 years old, of 16 stones still standing (there were 20) about ½-mile south of Carn Kenidjack (O.S. reference: 203/387324) and you may like to try and locate this relic of past ages. A track a few yards west of the Carn runs south to the stone circle.

The Penzance–St Just bus service serves Trewellard; also the rather infrequent summer service St Ives–Land's End.

MADGY FIGGY'S CHAIR

We owe the glorious coastal scenery of Land's End to the granite thrown up from some cataclysmic volcanic eruption many millions of years ago, quite a rare formation in England. Many of the vestiges of Cornwall's past history are due to its weather-resisting granite: the marvellous chamber tombs and other sites which could be over 4000 years old. But to the visitor the most spectacular aspect is the cliff scenery around Land's End. The pillars of rock, the cliffs pierced with innumerable caves and inlets, towering over 100 feet into the air, with the foaming seas below provide an unforgettable sight.

About 2½ miles south of Land's End by the Coast Path is Gwennap Head above which the Porthgwarra Coast Guard Look-out, one of the few manned night and day around the clock, is sited. A 'hole' on the top of the cliff nearby, formed by the collapse of a cave below, gives the name Tol pedn Penwith ('holed headland') to a lesser promontory and here will be found a rock pillar whose 'segments' give the impression of steps leading up to a 'chair' at the top. This is the Chair Ladder and sets the scene for the tale of Madgy Figgy's Chair.

St Levan, the small village the tower of whose church can be seen if you look east from the headland, was the home of the famous St Levan Witches of whom we hear about in the tale of Duffy and the Devil (see p. 108). The leader of the band was Madgy Figgy whose preference was for the sea. She would be seen at dusk on a stormy evening flying through the air to land like a huge black sea-bird on the 'Chair' of the Chair Ladder. She often had a lantern with her whose purpose was to lure passing ships to what they thought was a safe harbour but was in fact the inhospitable rock-girt beach of Porth Loe just north of the Chair. As the wretched crews tried, too late, to avoid being smashed to pieces on the rocks she

Porthgwarra – Madgy Figgy's Chair. (*Edmund Swinglehurst*)

would shout terrible curses and blood-curdling threats which terrified them even more and rendered them incapable of doing anything to save themselves. Once the wrecked vessels reached the shore the villagers, led by the Witches, would seize the plunder and carry it home, hastily burying any bodies on the cliff-top.

One stormy night a Spanish barque bound for the Netherlands from the treasure ports of the West Indies fell victim to Madgy's fiendish wiles. The splendid ship broke to pieces on the rocks and its crew, passengers and treasure were scattered over the length of the neighbouring coast. Bodies of richly dressed men and women were pitilessly rifled, the villagers loading themselves with fine clothes, silk and jewels which they hid in secret places until it was safe to sell them. Madgy Figgy, however, insisted that she would take charge only of the body of one particularly beautiful woman, finely dressed with many articles of gold and jewellery, and that her possessions should not be disposed of like those of the others. Some say that when Madgy turned the body over, the sight of the crucifix round its neck had such an effect on her that she insisted that if she and the others did not heed the message it brought there would be dreadful consequences. The lady was carefully buried in a special grave and her clothing and jewels locked in a chest in Madgy's cottage.

Strange phenomena began to be noticed. On moonless nights a strange ray of light seemed to hover above the lady's grave and travel over the ground until it rested on the chest in Madgy's cottage. It would then glide swiftly back to the grave and vanish. This occurred several times over a period of six weeks. One day a well-dressed foreigner appeared at the cottage. By signs – for he spoke no English – he somehow made Madgy and her husband understand he wanted to know where the graves were situated, and when shown he made his way alone unerringly to that of the lady, beside which he remained on his knees for a long time.

He then returned to the cottage and indicated he wanted

the chest to be opened. He took out the crucifix and what were obviously valuable personal pieces of jewellery belonging to the ill-fated lady. The rest of the contents he gave to Madgy to distribute among the villagers. He then walked slowly away.

Madgy claimed she sensed in him a fellow custodian of the forces of the unseen whom it would have been disastrous to disobey.

THE WALK:
FROM PORTHGWARRA
ROUND GWENNAP HEAD

MAP INSET
O.S. reference: 203/372217
Easy walk of 1½ miles – about 45 minutes, but can be extended at will along the Coast Path. Not suitable for Under Eights, in view of the unprotected cliff edges.

The little cove of Porthgwarra (Cornish: 'higher cove') is reached by a narrow winding secondary road from Polgigga on the B3315. Take the A30 towards Land's End and about ¾-mile before Land's End, the B3315 branches off to the left. Two miles down this road you come to the hamlet of Polgigga and a turning on the right with a signpost TO PORTHGWARRA (2 miles). Apart from the Coastguard Station and the Coastguard Look-out there are only a few houses in Porthgwarra but there is a small car park and, in the summer, a refreshment hut which serves teas. The beach is not really suitable for bathing; there is a fine rock arch on the beach.

Opposite the entrance to the car park there is a steep bank and on the left will be seen, close to a CAR PARK sign, the narrow entrance to a path which climbs the bank and leads to the cliff-top. Follow this. You will have a spectacular view of the rocky cliffs and the often turbulent sea. The route of the path is clear and passes to the seaward of two tall 'landmark' towers. The line of the two towers when extended out to sea marks the deadly

Runnel Stone, the 'moaning buoy' of which can be seen about a mile out to sea. The Stone has been the cause of many tragic shipwrecks. It used to jut further out from the waves but was broken off by a ship that was wrecked there.

The 'hole' through the cliff, an awesome sight, is below the landmark towers. Be careful how you approach the edge if you decide you want to look down to the sea below.

The path slopes downward above a small inaccessible cove, Porth Loe. Where the path levels out you can look back and see the pillar of rock – 'Madgy Figgy's Chair' – on which she used to sit. By taking the path which branches on the right up the slope you will come to the track which leads to the Coastguard Station (not to be confused with the Coastguard Look-out on the cliff) and back to the car park.

For those interested in birds, Porthgwarra is a famous place for spotting migrants in the spring and autumn. More than one rare species is usually seen here each year.

There are a few buses going to Polgigga on Service 504 from Penzance. Alternatively, there is a more frequent service to Porthcurno from which the active can walk along the Coast Path to Porthgwarra and have a look at the Minack Open Air Theatre en route – about 1½ miles of fine cliff walking each way.

THE LOGAN ROCK

A feature, both striking and puzzling, of the Cornish peninsula is the number of large rocks you are likely to come across – as part of the coastal scenery as well as inland – which precariously stand one on top of the other, always seeming to be ready to topple at any moment. The fact that they have been in that position for thousands if not millions of years does not prevent a slight feeling of alarm when you suddenly encounter one on the Coast Path or elsewhere.

Geologists will tell us, no doubt, that they were left behind in that state when the ice of some former Ice Age melted or when a primeval sea receded. It is said that some are so finely balanced that they can be rocked by hand, but volunteers ready to test this assertion are likely to be few, I should imagine. Quite a number of these 'rocking stones' or 'logans' as they are called (from the Cornish word for 'move') can be found when studying a large-scale map of Cornwall, but the best-known is the Logan Rock on the south coast of the Land's End peninsula, between Porthcurno and Penberth.

Logan Rock is the tip of the rocky headland of Treryn Dinas (Cornish – 'castle farm') and takes its name from a large square cushion-like rock, weighing 70 tons, which tops the 'last but one' pinnacle jutting out to sea. The Logan Rock has had a fascination for generations of Cornish folk. To climb up and give the Rock a push to make it move was thought to bring luck and couples would make the pilgrimage in the hope that obstacles in the path of their true love would by this means be made to disappear. But it was in 1824 that the Logan Rock became the centre of a first-class sensation.

During the April of that year, under the orders of their commander, Lieutenant Goldsmith, RN (nephew of the poet Oliver Goldsmith), the crew of HM Revenue Cutter *Nimble* came ashore with ropes and tackle and succeeded in toppling the Rock from its pinnacle. It is not recorded what the

Lieutenant's motive was for carrying out this strange operation: perhaps it was in a fit of frustration after a series of unsuccessful engagements with the smuggling fraternity of the area; or to punish the local populace for their lack of co-operation. Perhaps he wanted to give his crew some exercise and change of routine or it may have been just for a bet! We shall never know. Anyhow it turned out an expensive venture for him.

There was an immediate outcry when the news spread of the outrage inflicted on the Logan Rock. The attention of Lieutenant Goldsmith's superiors was drawn to his misplaced sense of duty and responsibility, and an order was issued that he should replace the Rock, at his own expense.

The task of hauling the 70-ton boulder of granite back to its accustomed place was a really formidable one. If you visit the spot you will see how it is almost inaccessible, with the narrowest of paths, and nasty drops either side for anyone missing their footing. To have to haul derricks, timber, tackle, etc., along these and then have to work in such a dangerous and confined space to assemble the tackle and muster as many men as possible to do the hauling must have been a hair-raising experience. We know it provided a fascinating attraction for the locals over many weeks.

The Morrab Library in Penzance has a copy of the account with the various items for which the unfortunate Lieutenant had to pay. They totalled £130.8s.6d, a sum equivalent to many thousands of pounds at today's values; they give an enlightening picture of wage rates and so on in that part of the country over 150 years ago. From the accounts it seems that it took from mid-September until November 6th, 1824, to mount the operation, replace the Rock and then dismantle all the tackle, etc. Fifty-eight men plus the crew of the *Nimble* managed over three days (October 29th–November 1st) to lift the Rock into place. The 'rate for the job' for the men was 2s.0d (10p) a day with masons getting 3s.0d a day. There was lodging to pay for '5 men for 18 days . . . £6', items such as

'Wm. Rawlings for drawing crabs and winches from Rock to Penberth . . . 10s.6d (52½p)' and others which must have upset young Goldsmith considerably . . . 'for 60 St Just men who did nothing but drink beer . . . 17s.6d (87½p)'! Those who are agile and clear-headed enough to walk out to the now safely lodged Rock (it does not appear to 'rock' nowadays) will find, if they look carefully, the holes that were cut in the surface of the supporting boulder to take the legs of the derricks; they may also notice other clues.

The whole affair was a nine days' wonder and Lieutenant Goldsmith became quite a hero, but I doubt if he thought it was worth it. He never rose above the rank of Lieutenant!

THE WALK:
FROM TREEN TO THE LOGAN ROCK AND PORTHCURNO

MAP INSET
O.S. reference: 203/395230
Apart from the scramble on to the Logan Rock itself, only for sure-footed adults, a pleasant cliff-top walk, 45 minutes each way, suitable for all, Under Eights included, if well supervised. Allow an extra 30 minutes for the scramble to Logan Rock and 30 minutes for a visit to Minack Open Air Theatre.

The start of the Walk is the quiet little hamlet of Treen, only ½-mile from the coast. It lies just off the B3315 road (from Penzance take the A30 and branch off on the B3283 via St Buryan. This joins the B3315 a mile from Treen). On the seaward side of the village there is an adequate car park and a small Post Office store. There is also a good pub, the Logan Rock which, together with a 2-mile stretch of coast between Treen and Porthcurno, is owned by the National Trust.

Logan Rock. *(Edmund Swinglehurst)*

By the car-park entrance and running by the side of an old chapel you will see a path, signposted TO THE LOGAN ROCK. You emerge at the base of the headland, Treryn Dinas, with some fine views of cliff and sea. Between you and the rocky tip of the headland bearing the Logan Rock lie the remains of a 'cliff castle', a Celtic fortification constructed between the third and first centuries BC. There are traces of a large rampart across the headland enclosing three smaller ones. At the 'neck' of the headland there was a ditch backed by a rock-faced bank. Traces of two huts have also been discovered.

If you are agile and sure-footed you can walk and scramble to the base of the Logan Rock, following a clearly discernible path.

Back to the National Trust sign at the end of the path from Treen. Turn westward (to the right, facing the sea) and continue along the Coast Path on the cliff-top. Porthcurno, the next village, used to be the terminal of the Eastern Cable Co's cable to India, and the Cable & Wireless Training College is still located there. The white pyramid you pass on the path is a navigation guide and also marks where the Transatlantic cable from Canada via France used to come ashore. If you look back from here at the headland, you should be able to see clearly the Logan Rock.

The path descends to the shining white beach of Porthcurno – composed of minute shells, not sand. From the beach a very steep flight of steps leads to the top of the cliff and the famous Minack Open Air Theatre founded by Miss Rowena Cade 40 years ago. The auditorium, facing the sea, is in a marvellous position with the whole of Mounts Bay as a 'backdrop' to the stage below. You may look over the theatre during the season on payment of a small charge. (Those not wishing to climb the steep steps up the cliff can reach the theatre by taking the road at the back of the beach which takes longer but is less steep.) Also of interest is the little disused house by the beach, built in the cliff by Miss Cade.

There is a large car park in Porthcurno.

The 504 Western National bus service runs between Penzance and Treen and Porthcurno on weekdays throughout the year and on Sundays in the summer season. Check locally.

THE SPECTRE BRIDEGROOM

Many visitors to the southern coast of the Land's End peninsula know of the famous Logan Rock which until it was dislodged 150 years ago had the reputation of being able to be rocked with one's little finger. It lies on the coast near the tiny village of Treen. Fewer people visit the small fishing cove of Penberth just a mile eastwards along the coast, preserved for ever for us by the National Trust. On the eastern slope of the little valley which leads down to Penberth cove lies the farm of Boscean which, at the time of our tale, about 250 years ago, was the home of the Lenine family: father, mother and the only son, Frank. The farm was a prosperous one and the father had hopes of being accepted into the higher ranks of the Cornish gentry, with his son not only inheriting the property but making it even more prosperous.

Helping the farmer's wife was Nancy Trevorgan, a young girl of remarkable beauty. Of true dark-haired Cornish blood, Nancy was not only beautiful but of sweet character. Her parents came from Ailsa, a short distance inland, where they had a small plot of land. Her mother had had a good education, for those times, and had passed on to Nancy much of her learning, of which the girl, with quickness and intelligence, took full advantage. She was accepted into the household of the Lenines and became more of a companion to Mistress Lenine than a servant.

She had not been working long at the farm before Frank fell deeply in love with her and, as he was a handsome and lively youngster, his love was returned. Every moment they could spare from their work they were together, and as they enjoyed the marvellous walks along the cliffs and over the shining sands of Porthcurno, they knew they were made for each other.

The time came for Frank to tell his father of his love for Nancy and that he wished to marry her. His father, who

Penberth. *(Edmund Swinglehurst)*

usually was quick to allow his son whatever he asked, this time refused and, sending for Nancy, ended her employment at the farm, sending her back to Ailsa.

This cruel blow only increased the love of the young couple. They continued to see each other, planning secret meetings: at dawn as Frank was on his way to the fields; at noon, when everyone was resting from the morning's work; at evening, snatching blissful moments behind the stone walls of the homeward path. Soon Nancy found herself with child. Her parents called on Farmer Lenine to beg him to let Frank marry their daughter but he still wouldn't hear of it. Fearing Frank would take matters in his own hands he took him on a pretext to Plymouth and had him taken on board a vessel bound for Australia, paying the captain to see he was left ashore there. Poor Nancy was sent to work at Kemyel Farm some miles away, the child being looked after by her parents.

Nothing was heard of Frank for the next three years.

Nancy had given up hope of seeing her love and when two of her friends at Kemyel suggested on All Hallows' Eve that she should join them in the ancient custom of scattering hempseed and by moonlight praying the spirits to reveal to them the future, she readily agreed. Nancy scattered her seed and saying three times the words prescribed asked that she should be shown her lover. Feeling a presence behind her she turned and glimpsed the apparition of a man which she recognized as her Frank. His face was a ghastly white and his hair was dripping wet. He gazed at her with piteous eyes and slowly disappeared. Struck with terror she rushed home and passed a sleepless night, her thoughts in a turmoil.

At the end of the following week there was a fearful gale and the alarm was given of a large vessel drifting towards the Merthen Rock near Penberth, the graveyard of many a fine ship. Unknown to Nancy and his father, on board this vessel was Frank Lenine, coming home at last. Nothing could be done to save the ship with such a wind driving her landwards, and with a crash of breaking spars and cries of those on board she struck the Rock. The local people rushed down to the cliff to try and save those washed ashore. Among the bodies they found someone who was just alive and they recognized him – it was Frank Lenine. He gasped out that they were to take him to Boscean where he could marry Nancy before he died. Hardly had they started on the way to the farm when he passed away. They buried him the next day in St Buryan Churchyard.

Nancy, who knew nothing of what had happened, was about to go to bed the evening after Frank's funeral when she heard the sound of horses' hooves outside and on going to see who it was, saw the horse that had been Frank's and a rider who, in the semi-darkness, was inviting her to get up behind him. Joyfully she recognized the figure of her lover but when she clasped the hand he offered it was as cold as ice, as was his body as she held on to his waist. The horse galloped off at a frightening speed with Nancy becoming more and more terrified. She saw that they were passing through St Buryan and that the door of the smithy was open. She cried to the smith to rescue her. He dashed out with an iron still red-hot in his hand and snatched at Nancy's dress as she flew past. The horse was brought to a halt and the ghostly rider pulled at the dress but the smith burned through the stuff. Nancy fell senseless to the ground and the horse took a flying leap over the churchyard wall and then was seen galloping towards the cliff, without its rider. Nancy was taken to Ailsa where she survived for only two days after her dreadful ordeal. The body of Frank's horse was found at the foot of the cliff.

THE WALK:
A CIRCULAR WALK FROM TREEN, OUTWARDS VIA THE COAST PATH RETURNING BY ROAD

MAP INSET
O.S. reference: 203/395230
A fine cliff walk and a visit to the unspoiled fishing village of Penberth. Allow 2 hours. Suitable for Under Eights if well supervised on the Coast Path.

The start of the Walk is the car park at Treen, as for the Logan Rock (see p. 100). From the car park you make for the Coast Path following the footpath signposted TO THE LOGAN ROCK. Where the path emerges on the cliff the line of the Coast Path should be clearly visible to your left and right. Take the left-hand (eastward) track. After dipping through the bracken and then up to the cliff-top (Treen Cliff) with splendid views, the path levels out for a stretch before descending steeply down to the picture-book fishing hamlet of Penberth and its cove. This is National Trust property as are most of the cottages in the valley. The Trust lets them to local fishermen who have formed a co-operative, and to those engaged in supplying the market with early spring flowers, etc. Thus is the community being preserved in its traditional form. There is no car-parking facility for visitors nor are there any shops or refreshment facilities. Skin-diving is not allowed. You can have your picnic on the cliff before climbing down to the cove.

For the return, take the road leading inland from the cove. There is little traffic and you can walk slowly admiring the granite cottages and their gardens, dallying at the bridge to gaze into the stream. You eventually reach the main B3315 road a few yards from the junction with the short approach road to the Logan Rock pub and the car park in Treen.

When you have your first view of Penberth and its wooded valley as you climb down the path from Treen, you may notice a house standing out among the trees halfway up the eastward flank of the valley. This is Boscean and may be the site of the Lenine family farm, scene of Frank and Nancy's romance.

Bus services as for the Logan Rock Walk, see p. 102.

DUFFY AND THE DEVIL

At the head of the valley which leads down to the delightful fishing village of Lamorna is the farm of Trewoofe. Its name means in Cornish 'the farmstead of the blacksmith' and is pronounced – and was sometimes spelt – 'Trove'. Many years ago the owner was a jolly, good-natured farmer called Squire Lovel and at the time of our tale he had been a widower for some years and had a half-blind, rather aged housekeeper.

It was his custom, when the cider-apples in his orchards were ripe, to ride over to the nearby village of Buryan to hire some of the young people to help with the cider-making: some to gather the apples, some to man the cider-presses, and some to help with the other jobs that needed doing at this busy time. He was on his way one fine autumn morning, when passing the cottage of old Nancy Tredwyn on the outskirts of the village he heard loud cries and there was old Nancy beating her stepdaughter Duffy, shouting between the blows: 'You lazy hussy! Where's the milk I told you to fetch and why isn't the kitchen swept? Your spinning and knitting is a disgrace. Take that! And that!' Now Duffy was a comely young girl and, in fact, did much prefer gallivanting with the boys to doing her chores. For Squire Lovel, like most men, a pretty face excused many defects and he stopped and urged Nancy to stop beating Duffy who, through her tears, protested to him that her spinning and knitting were as good as anyone's.

The Squire went on and engaged the young folk he required; on the way back he called at Nancy's and told her he needed a young girl to help the housekeeper to spin the wool and knit his stockings. He would like to take Duffy back with him. He was sure she would not mind as she was of so little use to her stepmother, apparently! So Duffy mounted up behind him and they made their way back to Trewoofe.

The next day the housekeeper led Duffy up to the attic where all the wool was stored, ready to be spun and knitted. After great elation at being taken to her new home at the Squire's pleasant farm, Duffy was in blackest despair as her spinning and knitting were really terrible and she could see herself being sent back to old Nancy's. 'The devil can do the Squire's cursed spinning and knitting, for all I care,' she shouted, aiming a kick at the heap of wool at her feet. Hardly had she spoken when she nearly jumped up to the roof-beams in surprise as a little man with chilling eyes dressed totally in black came out from a dark corner and said: 'Don't fret, Duffy dear. I'll help you with the knitting and spinning. You've no need to worry. Just make a wish when you want anything done and I'll see to it. I have one condition to make. Will you accept this?' Duffy, immensely relieved, vowed she would abide by any condition. 'Right then,' said he. 'After three years you will have to come with me unless, when the day comes, you can guess my name!' Our Duffy was the type who lived day by day and didn't let any possible future problems worry her, so she readily agreed. 'I'm off now,' he said. 'You can start wishing!' and vanished, leaving behind a slight smell of burning sulphur.

Of course, Duffy wished for some fine stockings for her master and there, at her feet, were four pairs of the most beautifully knitted stockings she had ever seen; when the Squire saw them he was overjoyed. He was even more contented when Duffy continued to supply him with more of equally good quality. Never had his legs been so dry and warm when out hunting in all weathers. Duffy even provided fine blankets and warm vests. He sang her praises wherever he went: on the hunting field; in the inns; and on coming out of Buryan church after service he was besieged by the ladies wanting to see his remarkable stockings. Pretty Duffy became much sought after by the local menfolk so Squire Lovel had to marry her to keep such a wonderful provider by him.

Now Duffy, who had plenty of time on her hands, was in

the habit of going down to the Mill to join the other women in a good gossip and perhaps a song and dance to while away the time. The miller's wife, Old Jane, was the life and soul of such affairs. She was also a witch, and unknown to Duffy had discovered her secret. The years soon went by and there was only one more day left. Duffy was now nearly out of her wits with worry. She resolved to ask Jane's help. 'How can I possibly guess his name?' she cried. 'What is going to happen to me?' Old Jane tried to comfort her. 'Go and fetch me a jug of the strongest beer from the Squire's cellar and when he goes hunting stay up until he returns, no matter how late it is, and don't interrupt him if he says anything to you!' Duffy ran and fetched the beer. 'Now. Remember what I told you,' said Jane. 'I'm off!' And so saying she put her shawl over her shoulders and headed for the high ground called Trewiden Moor, nursing the jug of beer.

Duffy went home and settled down to wait for the Squire. About three in the morning he burst in, covered with mud and wild of eye. 'Duffy, Duffy, what a day I've had! You'd never believe. I must tell you. Hardly found anything to chase all day until just as sun was setting I started the finest hare you ever saw. What a dance he led us. Down Lamorna Vale; up to Boleigh. Past the Merry Maidens until he disappeared down the Fogou hole. I followed down the hole with the dogs. On and on. And then suddenly we came out on a flat sward on which a fire was burning. And, would you believe it, a whole host of witches, Old Jane from the Mill included, were dancing and drinking, kicking up the devil of a row. There was a funny little man in black singing and dancing with them and Jane kept giving him more and more drink. He was really wild. He was singing a funny song:

Duffy dear, Duffy dear, with me you must now stop, stop.
You'll never guess my name: Terry Top, Terry Top, Top.

Then the witches saw me and with one accord they made for

me. I fled. Didn't stop till I reached here. What a night! Phew, I'm off to bed.'

Duffy hugged herself with joy. She had her answer. As soon as it was light she went to the attic. He was there, gloating. 'Well, Duffy dear. What is my name?' 'I don't know – can it be Beelzebub?' 'Never!' answered he. 'He's my valet.' 'Perhaps Old Nick?' 'Don't trifle with me, girl, or else it will be all the worse for you!' 'I believe it is Terry Top.' With a cry, a flame and a puff of sulphurous smoke he vanished and Duffy was free.

Unfortunately, at that same moment, the Squire who was out hunting felt a sudden chill. His wonderful stockings had disappeared and where was his vest? At home the blankets on the bed went as well. Of course, he blamed Duffy and gave her a very bad time. She had to flee to see Old Jane who luckily gave her some advice on how to get back into his good books again. I do not know what it was but it worked, I'm glad to say!

THE WALK:
FROM LAMORNA COVE
TO THE MERRY MAIDENS
STONE CIRCLE AND
RETURN

MAP INSET
O.S. reference: 203/450241
A walk through the charming village of Lamorna, then by footpath. Return the same way or follow a circular route. Allow 1 hour each way (1½ miles). Suitable for all ages.

The Walk will take you over some of the ground covered by Squire Lovel on his exciting hare-hunt. The Merry Maidens is the name given to one of Cornwall's best-known archaeological monuments. The Maidens are 19 large standing stones, 4–5 ft high in a perfect circle – there were originally 20. The age of the circle is uncertain but is not likely to be less than 3000 years. It lies in a field off the B3315 (O.S. reference: 203/433245).

Lamorna Cove is reached by a turning off the B3315 (Penzance) Newlyn–Land's End road. Follow this down the wooded valley, a lovely shady spot on a hot summer's day. You will find parking space on and near the quay of this former fishing village. There is a superb view over the sea and cliff from the quay.

For the Walk, proceed back up the valley. This will allow you to appreciate the beauty of the little stream and its woodland setting. Close to The Wink pub (mentioned on p. 119) there is a turning on the right which leads down to a well-preserved seventeenth-century mill which you may wish to see. Continuing up the road, beyond the turning place for the buses, there is, on the left, near a garden gate, a wide unmarked path going off at an angle. Turn up this right-of-way which leads past the entrance-drive of the Menwinnion Hotel, on to a by-road with a few houses (New Town) and a Wesleyan chapel, eventually emerging on a bend in the B3315. A yard or two along this road, there is a gap in the hedge on your left. This is the start of a footpath going diagonally across a field. This path cuts off the corner on the main road and continues to the next field by a stile. In the centre of this field stand the Merry Maidens.

Along the main road in the direction of Lamorna, in a field on the left, stand two 15-ft-high granite pillars known as the Pipers. The story is that the Merry Maidens were turned to stone for dancing on a Sunday to the tune of the Pipers, who suffered the same fate. Another tradition is that they commemorate the peace between the Cornish and the Anglo-Saxons under Athelstan in the tenth century after a battle nearby.

After seeing the Merry Maidens and the Pipers you can return to Lamorna by the same route as outward or if you prefer a circular walk, turn down the country road at the side of the Wesleyan chapel in New Town which you passed on the outward walk. This will bring you to Tregurnow Farm. Turn left at the Farm down the farm track. On reaching a metalled road, turn left and in a few minutes you are back on the road leading down to the Cove.

The Fogou down which Squire Lovel followed the hare is in the grounds of a private house in the neighbourhood. It is an underground chamber of large stone slabs. Fogous are a feature of this part of Cornwall; they were possibly used for storage and are reckoned to date from the first century BC.

Squire Lovel's house, Trewoofe, is still there, lying a short distance off the B3315, looking very much the same as it must have done 200 years ago.

Lamorna Cove is served by the Western National bus service 504 (Penzance–Porthcurno) on weekdays throughout the year and on Sundays in the summer season. Other buses on the same route call at Lamorna Gate on the main B3315 from where you have a mile walk down to the Cove. Check times, etc., locally.

In addition to The Wink pub there are refreshment facilities in the season down on the quay.

SOUTH CORNWALL (West)

The Smugglers of Prussia Cove

The Lord of Pengersick

The Poet of Godolphin House

Tregeagle

THE SMUGGLERS OF PRUSSIA COVE

Cornwall is always associated with smuggling, with reason, and near Cudden Point in Mounts Bay you will find Prussia Cove, favourite haven of Cornwall's most famous smuggling family, the Carters.

John Carter, born in the early 1700s, and his three sons – John, Charles and Henry – became the most successful smuggling partnership on the coast. Expert seamen, with a vast knowledge of the currents, rocks, shoals and landing places, they were able time and again to outwit His Majesty's revenue cutters which had the unenviable job of preventing the traffic in untaxed spirits and other contraband. John senior so prospered that he was able to build himself a substantial stone house – now long disappeared – on the cliff above Prussia Cove. This was used as some kind of inn which may have been called, like many other inns of that time, The King of Prussia after Frederick the Great, our popular ally in the Seven Years War, giving the name to the cove below; or, according to some, John himself was nicknamed The King of Prussia from his likeness to Frederick in form and personality.

Prussia Cove and the adjacent Bessie's Cove were particularly suitable for those in the smuggling trade, with long, narrow deep-water approaches and caverns for temporary storage. A path led down the cliff connecting with the road running inland. Bessie's Cove was said to be named after a Bessie Burrows who kept a small 'kiddlywink' inn on the cliff-top. We do not know exactly why Bessie was honoured by having the cove named after her. Perhaps only contraband liquor destined for her kiddlywink was landed and stored there. Incidentally, a kiddlywink is an inn with only a beer licence but by giving a nod and a wink you could get your tot of spirit from 'under the counter'. One of the few kiddlywinks remaining in Cornwall is the hospitable Lamorna Inn at Lamorna on the coast between Penzance and Land's

Prussia Cove. *(Edmund Swinglehurst)*

End. It is still known locally as 'The Wink' and if you look at its signboard you will see it depicts a winking customer.

John Carter senior had two ancient cannon mounted in front of his home and on one occasion, seeing the revenue cutter *Fairy* chasing and about to capture one of his smuggling vessels just off the coast, he fired on the cutter which fled. Brought before the magistrates he was discharged, having excused his conduct by saying he thought the cutter was a French privateer of which there were many cruising around at the time.

We can get an impression of the smugglers' exciting lives from the account written at the end of his life by 'Captain Harry' Carter, one of the sons. With their enterprises becoming more and more successful the Carters were able to build better, larger and faster ships. Harry on one occasion called at St Malo to pick up a cargo of spirits. While there he was caught up in a quarrel with the French who confiscated the ship and put himself and his thirty-six-man crew into prison. The fact there were thirty-seven on board is evidence of the size of the vessel. The prisoners were only released after a long stay in exchange for two high-ranking French prisoners held by the British. Harry's worst experience was when his ship was caught in Cawsand Bay near Plymouth by a revenue cutter. His vessel was boarded and he and his crew overcome in a fierce cutlass fight, Harry himself receiving severe head wounds. He was left for dead on the deck but although weak from pain and loss of blood he managed to heave himself over the ship's side into the water and struggle ashore. There he was found by his brother Charles who was looking for survivors. Charles took him back to Prussia Cove and hid him, as there was a reward of £300 on his head (over £20,000 by today's value). Hiding places were changed many times; one of them was Acton Castle (now a hotel, to be seen high up above the Coast Path west of Prussia Cove), built by one of the local gentry who, as was often the case, was in league with the smugglers.

Eventually they were able to get Harry away to Lisbon; from there he went to New York. In New York he came in touch with the Methodist movement and was 'converted'. Turning over a new leaf he decided to return to his brother's farm at Kenneggy. Before long he was warned that the authorities were after him again so he escaped to Roscoff in Brittany, one of the main sources of supplies of spirit, where he knew many of the merchants. Apparently he regarded selling liquor to his compatriots as allowable under his Methodist conscience. While he was at Roscoff the French Revolution broke out and all the British were imprisoned. Harry was not released until the end of the Terror in 1794. He came home once again and settled down at Rinsey Farm, a mile or so to the east of Prussia Cove, where he was apparently left in peace.

THE WALK:
DOWN TO BESSIE'S COVE;
ALSO A SUGGESTION FOR
A CIRCULAR WALK FROM
PRUSSIA COVE VIA THE
COAST PATH AND
TREVEAN

MAP INSET
O.S. reference: 203/555282
A short 10-minute walk down to the beach at Bessie's Cove; the circular walk along the Coast Path and home inland via Trevean (about 1½ hours: 2 miles) is not really suitable for Under Eights.

The car park above Prussia Cove is reached by a short secondary road of 1½ miles which turns south off the A394 Helston–Penzance road at Rosudgeon. By the entrance to the car park, directions point you to the footpath to Prussia Cove. The beach at Bessie's Cove is accessible, except at high tide, by means of a short, steep, narrow track. You can see where the boats of the smugglers could run close in, in deep water, and unload on to the flat rocks. The battleship the Warspite, *veteran of two world wars, was wrecked off Prussia Cove in April 1974; she was driven on the rocks in a storm when being towed to the breakers' yard; there is a pillar recording the event on the cliff near Cudden Point.*

For those with the time and energy a good circular walk may be enjoyed by joining the Coast Path above the Cove and walking westward past Cudden Point along the 100-ft-high cliffs, with excellent views of Mounts Bay and St Michael's Mount. The path climbs on the right (as you look out to sea), past a fisherman's hut where boats are often being painted and nets mended. After about 45 minutes' walking (1¼ miles), crossing two small streams, you come to a patch of grassy green sward on the right of the path. (The path, incidentally, keeps close to the cliff edge along most of the way; in case of doubt take the track nearest to the sea.) By this grassy patch you will see a grass cart-track leading inland on the near-side of a stone wall (on the seaward side of the Coast Path the cart-track leads down to the shore). Turn up the grassy track inland; this leads you in a few yards to an unmetalled farm road on the right; this is a right-of-way bringing you out at Trevean Farm. Follow the road round the farm to a metalled road. Almost immediately opposite you is a gap-entrance to a field, alongside two farm buildings one of which bears a warning notice, CATTLE CROSSING. The line of the footpath follows the seaward side of the hedge and across a stile into the next field. Follow along the landward side of this field-hedge to a metal gate with a stile. Cross the stile to a farm track which will bring you out on the road to Prussia Cove. Turn right and after ½-mile you arrive back at the car park. Be careful, as always, when walking down these narrow roads; keep in single file and face oncoming traffic.

The Falmouth–Helston–Penzance buses 502/3 maintain a good service (hourly weekdays; two-hourly Sundays) along the A394 to Rosudgeon. Ask to be put down at The Falmouth Packet.

There are no refreshment facilities at Prussia Cove but there is a good pub, The Falmouth Packet (with a small garden), on the A394 at Rosudgeon.

THE LORD OF PENGERSICK

The families who throng the beautiful sands of Praa in the summer little suspect the dramatic events which traditionally took place in Pengersick Castle (or Pengeswick as it used to be called), of which only a tower remains, just inland from the modern houses. The castle was erected by the first Lord of Pengersick about 300 years ago. He had made his money from the mining of tin and his ambition was to form an alliance with one of the famous West Country families and to found an aristocratic dynasty comparable to theirs. He planned that his only son, a young man of unusual intellect, should marry a lady of uncertain age, a connection of the Godolphins. This lady, as soon as she saw the wealth of the castle and its owner – and also the most handsome young man, his son – was equally keen on the idea!

Unfortunately the young man was not so eager. In fact he would have as little as possible to do with the lady and managed to escape from her embarrassing attentions. In desperation she went to see the Witch of Fraddon, whose magic powers were known to be the most effective in Cornwall. The Witch gave her many hints on how she could break through the young Lord's defences and gave her a selected love potion for his drink. To her chagrin everything proved useless. His delicate palate seemed to detect at once any interference with his drink and her other wiles had no effect. The Witch then sent her beautiful niece, Blitha, who was her usual assistant and as well versed in magic as her aunt, to the castle as a lady's maid to see what she could do. But, again, of no avail. As a desperate alternative the Godolphin lady decided to marry the old Lord.

Unfortunately Blitha fell madly in love with the young man who seemed to respond warmly although, as Blitha knew, there could be no question of her marrying him. The stepmother seeing them together, walking hand in hand over

Pengersick. (*Edmund Swinglehurst*)

the sands or climbing through the bracken of Rinsey Head, became mad with jealousy and plotted to get rid of the young Lord. She complained to her husband that he had forced his attentions on her and had suggested an illicit affair. Her suggestion was that he should be kidnapped and sold to the Barbary pirates who infested the foreign waters at that time. To reinforce her arguments she lied to the old man that she would soon bear him an heir.

Blitha, one of whose gifts was that of thought-reading, learned of this plot and warned her young lover. A fishing-boat was engaged to take him off secretly and safely to France.

A year or two afterwards the old Lord died and, strange to say, as though he had sensed the new situation, the young Lord of Pengersick arrived at the castle to claim his inheritance. But to everyone's amazement he was accompanied by a beautiful bride. She was of an olive complexion and they spoke together in some obscure Eastern language, she knowing no word of English. It transpired that in his travels, the young Lord had met the fate that had been planned for him earlier, had been captured by Barbary pirates and had been made a slave in the palace of a Bey. He had met Fatima, daughter of the Bey, who was versed in all the magic of the East. She taught him her secrets and together they used their occult powers to escape.

They were obviously deeply in love with each other and quickly took over the running of the castle. They found the stepmother shut up in one of the upper rooms and quite out of her mind. She would not talk to them and one day threw herself out of her window to the ground fifty feet below.

The young couple spent most of their time behind locked doors, engaged in occult experiments. Obnoxious smoke would seep from under the doors and weird cries came from inside as though wild spirits had been suddenly released.

Although the young master had a wild look in his eye and an air of mystery, Fatima was of a more gentle nature and when the bizarre experiments were at their height the strains of sweet music would be heard from the harp she played. Strange stories began to circulate and the servants went about their duties cowed and pale. The local people would not come near, and all stores had to be fetched from nearby Marazion.

In Marazion, a year later, a mysterious dark-skinned stranger was seen frequently in the streets. On one occasion he was heard asking the way to Pengersick and someone reported seeing him on Rinsey Head gazing fixedly down at the castle. One evening a red glow was seen in the sky to the east of Marazion and people streamed out on the road to see what was happening. It was Pengersick and the whole castle was blazing. The townsfolk could only stand shivering and staring as the stonework burst asunder with loud reports and the timbers fell in crackling flames. Soon the building was a pile of smoking stones. No one survived. The Bey's revenge was accomplished.

THE WALK:	MAP INSET
FROM PRAA SANDS	O.S. reference: 203/575282
TO RINSEY HEAD,	Allow 2 hours (3 miles).
RETURNING INLAND	Suitable for all ages.

Praa Sands (we are told that 'Praa' should be pronounced 'pray') lie 1 mile south of the A394 Helston–Penzance road, the turning being 6 miles from Helston and 7½ miles from Penzance. Our Walk will take us over the ground where Blitha, the beautiful witch, and the young Lord of Pengersick used to wander as in the story.

As you turn off the A394 and descend the slope leading down to the resort you will see a ruined tower on your right opposite a farm. This is the reputed site of the ill-fated Castle of Pengersick. There is very little room to park here at the side of the road; carry on down the main road (Castle Road) to the car park near the beach.

The sands are ideal for children. The first part of the Walk is along the sands – which stretch for almost a mile – towards the cliffs. Just before reaching the cliffs you will see an opening leading up from the sands to the cliff path and a National Trust sign LESCEAVE CLIFF. Follow the cliff path which takes you through a private estate to the top of the cliff. (For an interesting extension of the Walk, if you have time: continue along the cliff path for ¼-mile and you will come to the former Wheal Prosper copper mine which closed down over 100 years ago; the ruined engine house and chimney should make a good camera subject, with the background of Mounts Bay.)

Our Walk continues inland along the track leading from the top of Rinsey Head. You come to a large farm, Rinsey Farm; on the left is a PUBLIC FOOTPATH sign. Take this footpath across the fields and you come out shortly on to a narrow country road. Turn left, past the drive of the Lesceave Cliff Hotel. At the bottom of the hill there is an entrance to a right-of-way through an estate of elegant villas. This will bring you out on the turf-covered front of Praa Sands and back to the car park.

There is a good daily Western National bus service along the main A394 road: services 502/3 Falmouth–Helston–Penzance. Ask to be put down at Praa crossroads. Walk the mile down to the sands.

THE POET OF GODOLPHIN HOUSE

One of the most delightful experiences when exploring Cornwall is, to my mind, when you are crossing a rather austere part of the countryside, the road suddenly dips sharply and you find yourself among splendid trees and green fields with perhaps a river running through a valley. In such a setting stands Godolphin House just north of the Helston–Penzance main road.

This former home of the Godolphins, one of Cornwall's most famous families, dates from the seventeenth century although there was a house on the site much earlier. The most famous member of the family was probably Sidney, first Earl of Godolphin, Lord High Treasurer to Queen Anne and friend of Marlborough, but the one who interests me most is the young poet Sidney Godolphin. This Sidney was born at Godolphin in 1610 and after studying at Exeter College, Oxford, became MP for Helston. He travelled in France and the Low Countries and was a member of an official mission to Denmark. Small of stature he seems to have been regarded with affection by his contemporaries at Court, one of his fellow Cavalier poets, John Suckling, calling him 'Little Sid'.

In common with most of the Cornish families, the Godolphins rallied in support of King Charles when the Civil War broke out (although one of Sidney's cousins joined the other side). Sidney joined with the Grenvilles, Vyvyans, Trelawneys and the others in raising troops to fight for the King's cause in the West. Devon and Somerset declared for Parliament so the Cornish under Sir Bevil Grenville, grandson of the famous Grenville of the *Revenge*, prepared to march. Things went well at first for the Cavaliers in 1643. Against the odds a force under two of the most able of the King's officers, Hopton and Sir John Berkeley, routed a numerically superior body of Parliamentarians at Braddock Down, a few miles north-east of Lostwithiel, capturing 1200 prisoners, guns

Godolphin House. *(Edmund Swinglehurst)*

and money. The next step was to rob the enemy of the use of Plymouth and preparations were made to besiege that city.

News was received of a body of Parliament troops marching towards Plymouth so Grenville sent Sir John Berkeley ahead on February 8th while he followed with the main body of dragoons to challenge them. With Sir John rode Sidney Godolphin, who was already on Hopton's war council, with other leaders. The small advance party entered Chagford on the edge of Dartmoor not suspecting that the enemy had occupied the town a few hours earlier. They were attacked and seeing that they were heavily outnumbered prepared to cut their way out. As they clattered through the market-place a stray shot struck Sidney in the thigh. He cried out, 'O God, I am hurt,' and fell from his horse. He was carried to the porch of what is now the Three Crowns Inn and died, presumably from loss of blood and lack of proper medical attention. His friends carried him to Okehampton where he is buried in the church.

Chagford, Three Crowns Inn. (*Edmund Swinglehurst*)

The messages sent to his home testify to the shock and sorrow everyone felt and to the love they bore him. Wrote Grenville: 'he was as gallant a gentleman as the world had'; Hopton: 'as perfect and as absolute piece of virtue as ever our nation bred'. The tribute of his friend in London, that distinguished man later to be the Earl of Clarendon, best describes for us his character: 'There was never so great a mind and spirit contained in so little room.' History has not given him a place among the foremost poets of his time but a critic comments that 'his lyrics breathe the spirit of the early Caroline poets and their blending of gaiety and melancholy'. Perhaps had he lived to maturity he could have become another Milton.

Aubrey in his *Brief Lives* tells how Sidney Godolphin was much in love with his cousin Mistress Berkeley (was she the daughter of Sir John?) and maybe it was to her he wrote:

> Or love me less or love me more
> and play not with my liberty.
> Either take all, or all restore
> Bind me at least or set me free.

The subsequent story of the Cornishmen in the Civil War is also a tragic one: how they by sheer courage won the battles of Stratton and Lansdown (near Bath), but with severe losses including their finest leaders. As the current doggerel had it:

> Gone the four wheels of Charles' Wain*
> Grenville, Godolphin, Slanning, Trevanion
> all slain

but they fought on until in 1646 the gallant Hopton gave in and sailed for France. Sir John Berkeley surrendered the same year as did old Sir John Arundell at Pendennis Castle, Falmouth, after a long siege, the last Royalist stronghold in Britain to yield.

*Charles' Wain (Wagon) was the name given to the constellation better known as The Plough or The Great Bear.

THE WALK:	MAP INSET
A SHORT CIRCULAR WALK FROM THE ENTRANCE OF GODOLPHIN HOUSE AND A SUGGESTION FOR A WALK UP A NEIGHBOURING HILL	O.S. reference: 203/602318 For the first walk allow 30 minutes. For the second, Castle Pencaire, allow 30 minutes each way. Suitable for all ages.

To reach Godolphin House from the south, turn right at Breage on the A394 Helston–Penzance road. From north Cornwall take the B3303 from Camborne or the B3302 from Hayle to Leedstown. The turning for Godolphin is at Townshend.

Godolphin House is a fine example of the type of house built by the families of influence in Cornwall. Its attraction is enhanced by its still being lived in by the present owners, using the furniture and fittings of 300 years ago or more. Among the many pictures is a portrait of Sidney Godolphin, the poet. The House has featured in the Poldark *series and the* Master Class *musical concerts on BBC TV.*

After you have visited the House there is a short walk you can take through woods. On leaving the House turn right and cross over. A short way up the road you will find a path with a PUBLIC FOOTPATH sign. Walk through the woods until you come to a fork in more open ground. Turn left and it will bring you out on the road below Godolphin House. Turn left again and you will arrive back at your start after about 300 yards.

A further suggestion is a walk to the top of historical Castle Pencaire hill nearby. From Godolphin House follow the road south to Godolphin Cross village. Turn right at the village cross-roads and then left, after a mile, down the road signposted ASHTON. Along this road there is, on the left, an imposing white-painted thatched cottage, 'Castle Pencaire'. Some 150 yards farther on, at a sharp right-hand bend, there is a by-road on the left leading to some houses. Pull in here and you should be able to find space for your car.

The track to Castle Pencaire (650 ft), surmounted by its Cross, starts here. It is not a strenuous climb and you are rewarded by splendid views: to the Lizard in the south and towards Land's End on the west. The Cross is a memorial to the fallen of both world wars from the parish of Germoe whose church you can glimpse below the hill (well worth a visit). On the summit of the hill, near the Memorial Cross, are the clear outlines of a hill-fort of pre-Roman origin. Immediately to the north is Godolphin Hill, at the base of which is a disused engine-house and chimney of one of the Godolphin mines of which there were a number in the area, both tin and copper, some dating from the Middle Ages. It is astonishing how many innovations and discoveries there were in the small area around Godolphin. As far back as 1689 it was at the Godolphin Wheal Vor mine that gunpowder was first used in Cornish mining; in 1715 the first Newcomen's steam pump in the county was installed in the same mine. The first 'non-church' village school in Cornwall was started by the Duke of Leeds in the early 1800s (the Dukes of Leeds succeeded to the Godolphin estates in 1766).

Adjoining Castle Pencaire to the south is Tregonning Hill and it was at the site of a mine on this hill that the Quaker chemist from Plymouth, Thomas Cookworthy, in 1746 found traces of china-clay. This was the prelude to the discovery in Cornwall of the largest deposits of china-clay in the world and the source of one of our most valuable exports. On innovations, we must not overlook the far-seeing Godolphin who imported in 1730 the Godolphin Arabian horse, ancestor of all English racing Thoroughbreds. There is a picture of him in Godolphin House.

Godolphin House is open to the public: in May and June on Thursday afternoons 2–5 p.m.; in July, August and September on Tuesday and Thursday afternoons 2–5 p.m. Teas are served in August and September. (These are the arrangements at the time of writing. For confirmation ring Germoe 2409.)

There is one bus on Thursdays from Praa Sands and Camborne serving Godolphin. The daily weekday bus service

Penzance–Camborne calls at Townshend (1½ miles from Godolphin House).

On your way to or from Cornwall you may like to stop in Chagford, for refreshment or accommodation, at the Three Crowns Inn, a fine former (sixteenth-century) manor-house, with the porch where the dying Sidney Godolphin was laid.

TREGEAGLE

Undoubtedly the most evil figure of Cornish folklore, barring the Devil himself, is Tregeagle, squire many years ago of Trevorder near Bodmin. During his lifetime he was guilty of every infamy and his name was execrated throughout the West Country. As an employer and landlord he was cruel and pitiless; as a husband and father, an ogre, driving his wife and daughters to early graves. As a magistrate, he was without mercy and sent many innocent men to the gallows. There was no evil device which he would not use to gain money for his own ends. At last, as he drew near to eighty, he felt his end was near. Terrified of what might happen to his immortal soul as a result of his misdeeds he called in the Abbot of the nearby monastery and promising a large sum of money implored him to do everything in his power to save him from eternal damnation. The Abbot, after extracting from him a confession of the wrongs he had done to others and full restitution, promised he would see prayers were sent up daily after his death to intercede for his soul. He was buried with full Christian rites, his soul remaining in Purgatory until his sins were expiated.

It so happened that just after his death the courts of justice at Bodmin were hearing a case in which a complaint had been made of the misappropriation of property in the area. The defendant was quite innocent but was unable to prove his case as Tregeagle, while pretending to be his friend, had without authority sold his land leaving no documentary evidence behind. The poor defendant was beside himself with worry until it was suggested to him that Tregeagle's spirit could perhaps be raised to testify on his behalf. His informant recommended that he should consult a local holy man who was known to be an exorcist with considerable occult powers. This minister led him to the chancel of his church and drew a circle on the floor. After being assured by the young man that he had sufficient faith the minister intoned a secret rite and called out in a loud voice, 'Tregeagle! Stand forth!' and lo! there standing in the ring was Tregeagle. It was explained to him what was needed from him, so thinking this might help his soul to find rest, he agreed.

The next day, the young defendant, after the judge had consented to his calling a witness on his behalf, called Tregeagle to the box. What a sensation his appearance made! The judge turned white and a gasp of horror rose from those in court. The young man calmly drew from Tregeagle a confession of his forgery and produced the false documents; the defendant was then cleared of all blame and the sum appropriated by Tregeagle was ordered to be paid back out of his estate. The figure of Tregeagle walked to the door of the court and vanished.

After this sensational appearance the problem arose: 'What is to happen now to Tregeagle?' Long and earnest were the Abbot and other church dignitaries at their prayers and deliberations. In the end it was decided that the best thing would be to set this wandering soul an impossible task which would engage him for ever and thus preserve him from the Devil's grasp. They hit upon the splendid idea of setting him to emptying the nearby Dozmary Pool with a limpet shell with a hole in it, and so, amid much cursing and swearing, that was what he had to start doing.

The winter winds and rains howl over the rocky moorland surrounding the Pool and the Devil through these tried to wrench Tregeagle from his task, but he did not succeed. One day in midwinter, however, His Infernal Majesty whipped up a thunderstorm and whirlwind of unimaginable fury. Poor Tregeagle fled round and round the Pool keeping only just clear of the Devil's grasp. Then when he was feeling a sulphurous breath on the back of his neck he recalled that witches and devils cannot cross water so, cutting straight across the Pool, he flew on until, almost at the end of his endurance, he reached the chapel on the hill above Roche, 20 miles away, and dived through the little east window and stuck there, startling out of his senses the hermit who lived inside. Here, however, Tregeagle was safe but he remained there kicking and screaming for day after day for the Devil was tormenting the parts of him that were hanging outside the chapel. The hermit after some months of this during which he had tried in vain to calm the poor spirit, implored his Abbot that he should rid him of this terrible burden. Once more the Abbot and his holy colleagues put their heads together. Long were their sessions and many were the suggestions made and thrown aside until one bright monk cried, 'Let him try making ropes of sand!' 'What a good idea, my son,' said the Abbot. 'We'll send him to Padstow and he can see what he can do at the mouth of the river,' so there Tregeagle went and started on his hopeless task. No matter how hard he tried, whenever he had scooped up enough sand to mould into rope shapes the tide streamed in and washed them away. This went on for years until there was a mountain of sand at the river mouth and the people of Padstow implored the Abbot to take Tregeagle away as he was silting up the entrance to the harbour (at low tide you can still see the dangerous Doom Bar where so many fine ships have been wrecked).

The Abbot enlisted the aid of St Petroc who bound the spirit of Tregeagle in celestial chains and transported him to the mouth of the River Cober on which Helston stands. Here he was sentenced to be a kind of 'dredger', scooping up huge loads of sand and shingle from the banks of the estuary and carrying them on his back to Porthleven. Here he unloaded them on to the beach where the powerful tides soon swept them away.

One day Tregeagle was staggering on his way to Porthleven when his foot was caught in a branch of a tree which had been brought down by the river. He toppled and fell, spilling all the load into the river at its mouth. From that time on, a tremendous bank of shingle, now known as Loe Bar, has prevented the river from flowing into the sea and a beautiful freshwater lake (the largest in Cornwall), the Loe Pool, has been formed. One unfortunate result, however, is that Helston ceased to have an outlet to the sea for the shipping that used the town as a harbour and the Cober just runs into Loe Pool and seeps away under the shingle to the sea.

So once again Tregeagle was moved on, this time to a site where there was no one he could harm with his labours. The next occasion you are out on the cliffs near the Coastguard's Look-out at Porthgwarra south of Land's End in a tearing gale, with the waves crashing on the rocks below you, it may be the Devil trying to stop Tregeagle completing his task of sweeping the sea-shell beach of Porthcurno round Gwennap Head to Mill Bay 3 miles to the north. I think it is going to take Tregeagle a long time yet!

THE WALK:
ALONG THE WEST BANK OF LOE POOL TO LOE BAR, RETURNING BY COAST PATH AND INLAND ROAD

MAP INSET
O.S. reference 203/640260
A pleasant circular walk of about 2 hours, suitable for all ages.

Of the various scenes of Tregeagle's horrific activities the one that lends itself best for walking is the lake, Loe Pool, part of the magnificent Penrose Estate that lies between Helston and Porthleven. This Estate belongs to the National Trust, the Penrose family still retaining the right to live there. The Walk through the estate may be combined with a walk by the beach at Porthleven and, of course, you can have a picnic in the Estate or by the sea. In the Estate you are asked not to picnic in the fields but only where there are seats provided; these are sited so as to command the best views over the lake and woods.

The small car park serving visitors to the Estate lies just off the B3304 Helston–Porthleven road. Helston itself is on the main

A394 road between Penzance and Falmouth (Penryn). Note that the B3304 has two branches linking Porthleven with the A394. The best route for Penrose is the branch turning off the A394 just outside the town of Helston (the other branch of the B3304 turns off further west and would entail your driving through Porthleven).

Some 1½ miles from Helston on the B3304, as the road emerges from a deep wooded valley, near the top of the slope, there is a narrow road on the left, signposted LOE BAR, by an old white cottage. A few yards on the left, down this road, is the Penrose Walks car park.

The Walks are well signposted. You follow the one marked to Loe Bar, the route taking you at first through fields and by-passing the Penrose home. You shortly come to the dense woods for which the Estate is famous, the path leading along the west bank of Loe Pool. The Pool is known for the variety of its bird life, particularly winter visitors: duck, grebe, etc. The spring is the time for the birds of the woodland and reed beds but you are asked not to stray from the marked paths.

The path emerges at a Lodge by the sea, adjacent to the shingle bank, Loe Bar and the Porthleven beach. Walking time from car park to Lodge: about 45 minutes. You can return the way you came or, to make a circular walk, continue along the track from the Lodge, above the beach. Where the houses start, this track becomes a road (Loe Bar Road). Take the first turning to the right along this road and turn right again at the next junction. This will bring you back to the Penrose Walks car park. From the Lodge to the car park takes about 30 minutes. This path on the west of Loe Pool is suitable for push-chairs or prams.

If you would prefer to spend most of the time on the beach, with a short walk in the Estate, you could use the other Penrose Walks car park above the beach, about ¼-mile west of the Lodge (O.S. reference: 203/637246). You reach this car park by driving through Porthleven and taking the road on the east side of the harbour, continuing straight up the Cliff Road.

For those liking a long walk, there is also a public path on the other side of Loe Pool, enabling you to encircle the lake; there is also a path all the way to Helston itself! These paths are not suitable for prams, etc.

If you wish to see Dozmary Pool, which Tregeagle had the job of emptying, you could perhaps do this easily by making a short diversion on your journey to or from Cornwall as it lies very near to the main A30, between Launceston and Bodmin. Everyone knows the famous Jamaica Inn (O.S. reference: 201/184768) on the A30.

Almost opposite the Inn, a few yards to the south-west (i.e. towards Bodmin) there is a narrow secondary road. Follow this road for 2 miles and you will come to a sign TO DOZMARY POOL on the left-hand side of the road. There should be space to park your car on the verge. Five minutes' walk along the track will bring you to the Pool. You will then be able to say you have seen the Pool from where, traditionally, the arm of the Lady of the Lake appeared to catch Arthur's sword Excalibur thrown into its waters that winter's moonlit night by Sir Bedivere as his master lay dying.

The Western National Falmouth–Penzance buses 502 and 503 pass the entrance to the Penrose Estate. Ask to be put down at the nearest stop to the public (inland) entrance to the Estate.

SOUTH CORNWALL (East)

TRISTAN AND ISEULT

Tristan was the nephew of King Mark of Cornwall. He had been left an orphan in the land of Lyonesse when his mother Blanchefleur, beloved sister of King Mark, died after giving him birth on hearing the tragic news that her husband, Rivolen King of Lyonesse, had been killed in battle against an invader. King Mark had him brought to Cornwall where he treated him as though he was his own son.

Tristan grew into a fine youth. He was without rival in hunting skill and with the sword and lance. With his harp and singing he charmed everyone. Four of Mark's barons were jealous of Tristan and, fearing the King would make him his heir, badgered him to marry so that he could have a son to succeed, threatening to transfer their allegiance to a neighbouring hostile King. One day as he was listening to their remonstrances a swallow flew in at the window of the palace bearing in its beak a golden hair which flashed in the sunlight. Said Mark, hoping to set an impossible task, 'If anyone will find me a maid with hair as golden as that brought in by this swallow, I will marry her.' Tristan, who was attending the King, told of the King of Ireland's daughter, Iseult of the Golden Hair, about whom an Irish mariner had told him: 'She is lovely of face and figure and her long tresses are as spun gold.' Mark ordered Tristan to take a hundred knights and the finest of his ships and bear a message to the King asking for Iseult's hand.

The King of Ireland received King Mark's request kindly and asked his daughter if she would be ready to marry the King of Cornwall. He gave her some days to think the matter over, during which time Tristan and his companions were feasted and took part in many jousts. Finally she gave her assent and in a splendid procession, escorted by his hundred knights, Tristan led her down to the ships.

Unknown to Iseult, the Queen her mother, had entrusted

Brangien, her daughter's maid and companion, with a powerful love-potion. 'Take this secretly and see that Mark and Iseult, unknowing, drink it on their wedding night,' she commanded. 'They will then be bound in eternal love until their lives' end.' As their ship, escorted by those bearing the knights, made its way in a strong favourable wind towards Cornwall's coast, while Brangien dozed, Iseult, feeling weary, asked Tristan for something to drink. Seeing the flask at Brangien's side he took it and offered it to her. She took a long drink and passed the flask to him. He also drank deep. Brangien woke and seeing the empty flask told her mistress what a terrible step she and Tristan had taken. The couple gazed at each other helplessly and, as they gazed, felt a surge of love take charge of their whole being. By nightfall they were drawn irresistibly into each other's arms and the sea and the sky around them seemed to cease to exist as they kissed. Came the morning and Tristan and Iseult had sworn a deathless love for one another. With agonized self-control they managed to hide their true feelings from their companions. Brangien pledged herself to keep their secret and to help them.

The ships arrived at their destination soon afterwards and Iseult was greeted by King Mark and the lords and ladies of the court. Everyone was enchanted by Iseult's beauty and grace and the wedding was celebrated with splendour at the Minster. The tormented lovers played their expected parts but, with Brangien's help, they met regularly in an orchard just outside the palace walls and gave themselves over to love.

Although King Mark, blinded perhaps by love for Iseult, suspected nothing the barons watched the couple closely and soon discovered their secret. They told the King what they had found and suggested he should hide in the branches of a tree in the orchard. Tristan, coming first to the tryst, hearing a movement saw the King and by signs warned Iseult they were being watched. The King then revealed himself. Iseult protested her innocence saying they had heard the rumours of the court and had arranged to meet to discuss how they could prove them unfounded. Mark's suspicions were allayed. The barons then decided to lay a trap. They persuaded Mark one night to give sudden orders to Tristan to take a message to a neighbouring king, knowing that Tristan would have to warn Iseult. They laid a track of flour and showed the King in the morning how Tristan's steps had led to Iseult's room.

The couple were seized and brought before the King. They denied their guilt but Mark's judgement was instant; death by burning. As they were being marched away to the stake a crowd of lepers begged the King to let them have Iseult to kill her in a more terrible way. He consented and she was dragged away. Tristan, on passing a chapel, begged his guards to let him make a last act of contrition. They consented and once inside the chapel Tristan leapt through a small window which opened to a sheer cliff hundreds of feet above the water. Believing he had no chance of survival, his guards left him. He *had* survived, landing on soft sand at the water's edge, and there he was found, unharmed, by his faithful steward, Gorvenal. Together they found Iseult and, attacking the lepers, rescued her and fled to the deep woods of the forest of Moresk some miles away.

Here in the woods, wandering from place to place to avoid detection, the lovers spent the autumn and winter. Tristan built rough shelters and caught game and by collecting berries and wild fruit they somehow survived. Their love gave them courage and endurance but they were deeply conscious of the wrong they had done King Mark. They sought the counsel of the Monk Ogrin who had his cell in the forest and, filled with remorse, decided that Iseult should go back and Tristan wrote a letter to Mark telling him of the love-potion they had taken in error and how it had entrapped them in an inescapable net of love. Tristan with breaking heart put Iseult on the road to the court, swearing that if ever she was in need of him he would fly to her. He resolved to wander, offering his services to whoever would welcome them. King Mark, with Christian magnanimity, took Iseult back to his heart.

In Brittany Tristan helped Duke Noel and Kehardin his son to defeat an attack from their enemy, Count Reol. In gratitude Noel gave him the hand of his daughter, Iseult of the White Hands, in marriage. Tristan tried to be a true husband but his wife sensed from the start that there was no room for her in his heart and that, as everyone had told her, his heart and life were still Iseult's of the Golden Hair. In a battle Tristan was wounded by a poisoned spear and became desperately ill. Calling Kehardin, Tristan gave him his love's jasper ring and bade him take it to Iseult at King Mark's court saying he was in need of her. 'I shall be looking out for your return,' he said. 'If you bear my love with you, so that my joy should not be delayed hoist a white sail, but if not, show a black sail and let me die.'

Kehardin hastened to Cornwall and gaining entrance privately to Iseult's chamber gave her Tristan's message, showing her the ring. 'I will come straightway,' she said and they ran back to his ship, setting sail for Brittany. As they came within sight of the Breton coast Kehardin hoisted the white sail to show Tristan his love was on her way. Iseult of the White Hands had however overheard the instructions he had given and was watching out for the ship's return. 'The ship is in sight,' she told Tristan. 'Is her sail white or black?' he asked. 'Black,' lied Iseult, revenging herself for the lack of love he had shown her.

On hearing her words, Tristan turned his face to the wall and died. Iseult of the Golden Hair, rushing in later with joyous expectancy, on seeing his corpse gave a shrill bitter cry and, falling down by his side, she too expired.

Their bodies were borne back to Cornwall with deepest mournings. King Mark ordered the most costly of funeral rites and they were buried side by side in coffins of chalcedony. A sweet briar was planted on each of the graves and it is said that, as they grew, their branches twined together.

'Is there any truth in the Tristan and Iseult legend?' is what we all ask ourselves. Historians and others have been puzzling over this for a long time without having been able to find any concrete evidence. On the other hand, those who make a study of Cornish place names have been able to identify some localities mentioned by the early chroniclers and, by comparing geographical features described in the story, have produced some intriguing theories.

The most authentic-sounding traditional link to my mind is the one which places the 'palace' of King Mark at Castle Dore, 2½ miles north of Fowey on the B3269. A few yards on the right (eastern) side of the road, past the crossing of the Golant and Tywardreath roads, there is a gap in the hedge and this leads to a large area surrounded by high grassy banks – the remains of a considerable rampart system. This is Castle Dore where research some time ago has shown that a settlement existed there since 200 BC and in later Celtic times. There are traces of a sizeable wooden structure which some experts think may have been King Mark's 'palace'. An inscription on the site gives more details. There are wide views from the 'castle' and in fine and warm weather it could be a pleasant spot for a picnic.

The possible connection with King Mark is supported by the deciphering of the inscription on a large upright stone monument which used to stand near Castle Dore and has now been set up on the left (east side) of the A3082 into Fowey just beyond where the B3269 joins it. The inscription is said to have read: 'Drustans hic jacit Cunomori filius' ('Here lies Drustan son of Cunomorus'). Drustan is an alternative name for Tristan and a Breton ninth-century chronicler mentions that 'Cunomorus' was another name for King Mark. The legend certainly says that Tristan was the nephew, not the son, of King Mark but one can easily

Castle Dore. *(Edmund Swinglehurst)*

appreciate that a pious monastic chronicler might want to switch the relationship to lessen the 'sin'. An explanatory tablet has also been set up here to elaborate the story. Another point of interest is that the B3269 is on the line of the ancient trackway leading from Padstow to Fowey. Padstow would be from early times a harbour with links with Ireland. Perhaps Tristan conducted Mark's beautiful bride along this trackway.

The church of St Sampson in Golant, about a mile down the road from Castle Dore, is said to have very early monastic origins and to have been the church where Mark, Tristan and Iseult worshipped. It is well worth a visit. To reach the church you must use the road; the right-of-way (a footpath) which would cut off a corner and is shown on some Ordnance Survey maps seems to have disappeared. This is being investigated.

One writer points out that the chapel where Tristan escaped through the window could well have been the chapel

Castle Dore. *(Edmund Swinglehurst)*

which stood on St Catherine's Point, Fowey, only 3 miles from Castle Dore. The cliff is so sheer here that he would certainly have fallen straight into the sea and thus have preserved his life.

Our main walk, however, has as its setting Tristan and Iseult's life of exile in the woods, after they had escaped the fearful deaths to which they had been condemned. The early chroniclers have left one or two clues and I am indebted to E. M. R. Ditmas's book *Tristan and Iseult in Cornwall* for the fascinating suggestions which follow. Basing her theories on the account of the twelfth-century Breton monk Beroul she gives as her opinion that the lovers took refuge in the thick woods that still fringe the Tresillian and upper Fal estuaries in the parishes of St Michael Penkevil and Philleigh. Mention was made in the twelfth-century account that Tristan and Iseult had to use a ferry to reach the woods where they were to hide and that the ground near the ferry was marshy. The place name of Blanchelande is quoted, which could be Nansavallon, near St Kea. There is the hamlet of Malpas, only 2 miles from Truro, where the Tresillian, Truro and Fal rivers meet, whose name signifies 'bad crossing', and which was the terminal for ferries to St Kea and St Michael Penkevil (only the latter is still running).

THE WALK:	MAP SQUARE C7
FROM MALPAS TO	O.S. reference: 204/845428
ST CLEMENT AND BACK.	A very pleasant walk by
ALSO A SUGGESTION USING	footpath, about 30 minutes
THE FERRY MALPAS–	each way, through fields and
ST MICHAEL PENKEVIL	over a hill. Suitable for all.

To reach Malpas, in its beautiful setting high above the Truro and Tresillian river estuaries, turn left (south) at the roundabout on the A39 as you enter Truro from the east. The turn-off is signposted. The hamlet lies 2 miles down this secondary road. Parking space is limited, particularly at weekday lunch-times in the summer when business folk from Truro congregate to eat their lunch in the sunshine at the excellent pub, The Heron. For the Walk, continue along the road past The Heron and where the road starts to turn away from the estuary towards an estate, on the right will be seen the entrance to a footpath running between two gardens. There is a sign: FOOTPATH TO ST CLEMENT. After a short stretch through a wood bordering on the estuary and over a stream, the path enters a field and climbs quite steeply over a grassy hill and down to St Clement following a well-marked route. The medieval castle of Moresk, of which nothing remains, was sited 500 yards east of the path on the grassy hill. It was traditionally an Arthurian stronghold. St Clement is in the quietest of backwaters, on the bank of the Tresillian estuary, with its bright flowers during most of the year forming a foreground for the lovely fifteenth-century church with its unusual house built over the lych-gate. In the churchyard is one of Cornwall's most valuable Cornish Crosses, with a Latin inscription. This is reckoned to be sixth century and when found was being used as a gate post on the vicarage site. If you would like to walk farther, a path leads along the bank of the estuary from St Clement for 1½ miles, emerging on the A39 near Pencalenick. You have fine views of the woods on the opposite bank and there are usually, at low tide, flocks of wading and other birds, seen at their best in the spring and autumn migrations. The estuary also has a number of wintering waders. Birds to be seen (according to season): curlew, redshank, greenshank, dunlin, oystercatcher, bar- and black-tailed godwit, etc., and you may be lucky enough to see a kingfisher.

For another Walk 'in the steps of Tristan and Iseult' take the ferry across from Malpas to St Michael Penkevil. You must ring the ferryman's bell on the landing stage at Malpas and the ferry will come over from the other side (daily except Fridays) to pick you up. From the ferryman's charming cottage the path leads up to the road which will take you to the impressive church of St Michael Penkevil (about 1 mile), in the quietest possible settings among a few cottages. Much of the church dates from the thirteenth and fourteenth centuries, with brasses of the fifteenth and sixteenth centuries (permission needed to take rubbings).

There is a weekday bus service (three buses a day: two on Saturdays) from Truro (The Green) to Malpas.

There are no refreshment facilities at either St Clement or St Michael Penkevil.

ST GERENNIUS

On the stretch of coast between Falmouth and St Austell Bay there are a number of places connected with a figure of Cornish legend who may have been an historical personage: King Geraint of Cornwall. Other variations of his name are 'Gerennius' and 'Gerendus' (to whom the church at Gerrans is dedicated, giving the name to the village). Sir Geraint, it will be recalled, was one of King Arthur's knights. The village of Gorran Haven is also one of those whose name is connected with the king or saint.

Scholars have searched and are still searching for more traces of Geraint's existence: theories place his court in the neighbourhood of Gerrans. On the map, 1½ miles north-east of Gerrans, just off the A3078 is marked 'Dingerein Castle' (O.S. reference: 882375) where, in a field, there is an earthwork. 'Dingerein' is Cornish for 'Geraint's Castle'. Another possibility is the site of the farm at Tregairwoon, north-west of Dingerein. 'Tregairwoon' means in Cornish 'farm near the camp on the moor'.

One of the legends of St Gerennius concerns his meeting with the Welsh saint, St Teilo. Teilo was Bishop of Llandaff in the seventh century. A fearful pestilence, the 'yellow plague', was devastating South Wales, claiming hundreds of lives and St Teilo decided to lead many of his flock to refuge in Brittany where his good friend, St Samson, another Welshman, had settled and had built a monastery at Dol.

The party set off, travelling through Cornwall, and came to the court of Gerennius, King of Cornwall, who gave them a great welcome. Gerennius was much uplifted by the presence of the saint from Wales and asked if he would hear his confession and give him absolution, to which Teilo gladly agreed. Gerennius then prevailed upon Teilo to promise that when he, Gerennius, approached the end of his life, Teilo would come and administer the last rites. Teilo and his companions then took sail to Brittany where they stayed for seven years.

When they were making preparations to travel back to their homeland Teilo had a dream in which Gerennius called to him from his death-bed and reminded him of his promise made seven years before. Teilo then ordered a stone coffin to be taken with them back to Cornwall. When his companions protested that their boat would be likely to sink if it were taken aboard – ten oxen were needed to drag it to the shore – St Teilo told them to tie it to the bows of the boat so it could float ahead of them on the water. To the astonishment of all, the stone coffin floated, as the saint said it would.

They were midway across the Channel when they met a boat coming in the opposite direction. As it drew alongside they recognized two of Gerennius's chieftains among the crew. They were bound for Brittany as their king, Gerennius, was dying and had sent for St Teilo. They bade Teilo to hasten.

Teilo landed and, to the joy of King Gerennius, reached his bedside and was in time to administer the Last Rites to the saintly King. Gerennius's body was embalmed and placed in the stone coffin Teilo had brought. Amid the lamentations of all his subjects the King's body was then taken in a boat, whose sides were plated in gold, and rowed across Gerrans Bay by oars covered in silver, to Pendower and hauled by a team of oxen with harness of silver to the height of Carne Beacon. There he was buried. The impressive burial mound (or tumulus) is still there to be seen, dominating the peaceful scene for miles around.

Those of you who know Brittany and possibly spent a holiday there may be interested to know that St Teilo's friend, St Samson, was one of the most famous of Celtic saints. The son of a wealthy Welsh family he was converted to Christianity and travelled to Brittany, there to found the monastery at Dol. The present thirteenth-century cathedral in Dol is dedicated to the saint, and the Bishop of Dol is regarded as the spiritual head of all Brittany. In Cornwall, the church at Golant near Fowey (see the legend of Tristan and Iseult on pp. 143–50) is dedicated to St Samson, and there is also the island of Samson in the Scillies and the town of St Sampson in Guernsey.

THE WALK:
ROUND NARE HEAD, WITH FINE VIEWS OF GERRANS BAY. PLUS AN OPTIONAL SHORT SIDE-TRIP EN ROUTE TO SEE THE BURIAL MOUND ON CARNE BEACON.

MAP SQUARE C7
O.S. reference: 204/921381
1 hour's walking time. Take your own food and drink.
Suitable for all ages, provided the youngsters are well supervised.

The start of the main Walk is the small National Trust car park serving the National Trust Nare Head property. Make for the A3078 Tregony–St Mawes road and take the turning to Veryan. From Veryan follow the sign TO PENDOWER where there is a good beach, with limited parking. To reach the Nare Head car park from Pendower Beach, your road climbs steeply from the east end of the beach. A mile down this winding road you will see Tregamenna Manor Farm on the right. Take the next (unmarked) turning on the right. The start of this farm road is obscured on the O.S. Map 204 but is at the point of the first letter 'a' of 'Tregamenna' (O.S. reference: 204/922389). After ¾-mile the farm road brings you to a farm and the National Trust car park.

Leave your car here and walk down the farm track which continues towards the sea. The track soon reaches the cliff, joining the Coast Path. Turn right (westwards) along the Coast Path which follows roughly the line of the cliff to Nare Head and then eventually reaches the top of a steep downward slope from where there is a splendid view of Gerrans Bay and the coast. Descend the steep slope, at the bottom of which you will see a footbridge crossing a small stream. Just before reaching the stream with its footbridge, turn right (inland) up the footpath which climbs gradually through a delightful small wooded combe. Cross over a stile and continue straight ahead along the edge of the field in front of you. Across a stile alongside the farmyard and you are back in the car park.

For the burial mound (shown as 'tumulus' on O.S. Map 204) on Carne Beacon follow the road, mentioned in the first paragraph above, rising steeply from the east end of Pendower Beach. Shortly after the road levels out at the top of the slope there is a sharp right-hand bend. At the 'elbow' of this bend (O.S. reference: 204/913386) there is a PUBLIC FOOTPATH sign to Churchtown Farm. Some 100 yards along this footpath is the large mound traditionally said to be St Gerennius's burial place.

The only bus route of any help in getting to the Nare Head car park is the one operated Truro–Portloe on certain weekdays by Roseland Motors. This will take you to Veryan, a 2-mile walk from the car park. The Truro terminus is The Green, where details should be available.

BODRUGAN'S LEAP

The Wars of the Roses (1455–85), between those supporting the claims of the descendants of one or other of the sons of Edward III: John of Gaunt, Duke of Lancaster (Lancastrians) and Edward, Duke of York (Yorkists), although immensely costly in lives and property – 100,000 are said to have died – was largely a war of the private armies of powerful noble families who ranged themselves behind the leader of their choice and, marching up and down the country, engaged each other intermittently in bloody conflict while the rest of the population looked on and prayed they would not be implicated. One of the healthy results of the struggle was that the power of these noble families – the Nevilles and Percys from the North and the Mortimers from the Welsh borders, and others – was broken for ever, as by killing each other off and impoverishing themselves in the effort, they kept King and Parliament stronger and the country easier to govern.

Although the south-west of England was not heavily involved in the Wars it was not completely unaffected. The important families of Cornwall and Devon, often having links with, or offices under, the reigning monarch, had to decide their allegiance when the throne was challenged – power changed hands three times between Yorkists and Lancastrians during the 30 years – and when their patron was toppled, suffered accordingly.

One of those who suffered in this way was Sir Henry de Bodrugan. Sir Henry belonged to one of Cornwall's oldest families – there is evidence of an Otho de Bodrigan leaving for a pilgrimage to Santiago de Compostela in Edward II's reign, the early fourteenth century. The family held lands on the high ground just south of Mevagissey. Bodrugan Barton ('barton' means farm and is derived from the Old English for 'barley enclosure') still stands on the spot where there must have been a large mansion 500 years ago.

Bodrugan Barton. *(Edmund Swinglehurst)*

Sir Henry was a supporter of the Yorkist King, Richard III – the Yorkists had been in the ascendancy for most of the period of the Wars of the Roses. He was apparently quite a character. He had the reputation of being hot-tempered and was always picking quarrels with his neighbours. He was, however, a generous man and his own people were very fond of him. He fought at Bosworth in 1485 where Richard met his death. He retired to his estates, but Henry VII, the Lancastrian victor and first of the Tudors, issued in February 1487, an order for his arrest and sequestration of his estates. Sir Richard Edgcumbe, member of another powerful West Country family (their magnificent Mount Edgecumbe estate opposite Plymouth Sound is now open to the public), was entrusted with the serving of the order.

Bodrugan must have been warned of what was happening and just had time to see that a boat was made ready and then slipped down to the water a mile away. The chase must have been hot as tradition has it that he had to jump 100 ft from the top of the low cliff to a grassy slope below near where the boat was waiting. He survived the leap and escaped to France and then to Ireland. The Edgcumbes took over his estates – at the end of last century they still owned Bodrugan Barton. Since Sir Henry's famous jump to freedom the spot has been known as Bodrugan's Leap. This section of the cliff is now owned by the National Trust: when you walk over the ground there seems to be more than one place where he could have jumped – you can make your choice.

One other incident of the Wars occurred in 1471 when the Yorkist Edward IV regained the throne after the second battle of Barnet. The Earl of Oxford, after escaping to France, returned in 1473 with a small squadron and captured St Michael's Mount. With 80 of his men, he was besieged by Sir John Arundell, a member of another of the great Cornish families, with 6000 men who were defied for six months. The lovely sixteenth-century home of the Arundells at Trerice near Newquay is now owned by the National Trust and may be visited.

THE WALK:
FROM PORTHMELLON NEAR MEVAGISSEY TO BODRUGAN'S LEAP WITH AN ALTERNATIVE CIRCULAR WALK TAKING IN BODRUGAN BARTON

MAP SQUARE C/D6
O.S. reference: 204/016438
A pleasant walk suitable for all ages. To Bodrugan's Leap from Porthmellon: about 45 minutes. For circular walk: about 3 hours. Add 20 minutes each way if starting from Mevagissey. Take your picnic with you.

Porthmellon is a small hamlet adjoining Mevagissey to the south. Mevagissey is reached from the A390 by the B3273 from St Austell. Porthmellon has a small beach, which is covered at high tide. There is limited parking for cars and you should get there early to be sure of a space. The Rising Sun pub in Porthmellon allows public parking in their car park, on payment of a charge. This facility may be suspended in July and August. Otherwise you should park in Mevagissey and walk along the road to Porthmellon (there is a footpath for 200 yards alongside the road where it climbs out of the town). From Porthmellon continue past the beach. After the road turns inland up the hill, take the turning on the left, Chapel Point Lane (Coast Path), which runs past some bungalows before coming out into the open. From there it is a fine cliff-top path leading down towards Chapel Point on which there is a large house. Before reaching the house the path branches to the right down to Colona Beach. On the rise the other side of the beach is the National Trust sign BODRUGAN'S LEAP, with the path continuing along the low cliff – a most pleasant spot. When the sea is calm swimmers can bathe off the rocks here. You can speculate where Sir Henry made his leap. One wonders why he did not choose Colona Beach to embark. Perhaps it was too open and under surveillance.

For those who want a longer walk, continue along the Coast Path until you come to the outskirts of Gorran Haven. As you reach a new estate, after passing a few houses there is a turning on the right going inland with a footpath sign on the corner TO TREWALLOCK. Go up the road until just before it turns left, where there is a narrow path beside a private garden. Follow this behind the houses; it emerges into open country, leading across a field to Trewallock Farm which you will be able to see ahead of you to the left. The path leads through the farm on to the road. Turn right along the road (as on all roads, take special care) and you will come to a road junction. Keep straight on and about 100 yards down on the right there is a footpath. This takes you across a field, with fine views, and on to the road again. After a few yards there is the farm entrance to Bodrugan Barton. Although there may not be a signpost on the roadway there is a right-of-way through this entrance (you will see a few yards farther on a direction sign as you come to the farmhouse on your left). Follow the directions through the gate, and there is a good path following the valley of the small stream down to Colona Beach to join the Coast Path to Porthmellon and Mevagissey.

There is a frequent daily bus service between Mevagissey and St Austell, which is linked by bus or train with Truro, Falmouth, etc.

FOWEY

1. PIRACY AND PIETY

I always think that Fowey is one of the most attractive towns in Cornwall – and that is not without due appreciation of all the other delightful spots in that county. It is not only the charm of its precipitous narrow streets with their old shops and buildings and the little quay that seems to have been built so that the locals can take their ease thereon, enjoy the view and gossip without being interrupted by transactions of tiresome business; nor the impressive church with the old manor-house only a few yards away, right in the middle of the town. It is its air of dignity justified by a tradition that goes back 800 years – it was granted a charter in 1200 – and a sense of having played a dramatic, although not always respectable, part in the history of the south-west.

The 4000-year-old urn and Roman coins in Truro Museum which were found on the slopes above Fowey provide evidence of very early habitation but it seems that the settlement grew in importance after the departure of the Romans in the fifth century. Fowey was the southern terminal of the ancient trackway across the peninsula from Padstow. A result of the invasion through eastern Britain by Saxon hordes was that the Romano-British, driven to the western 'fringe' and surviving there for some hundreds of years in Cornwall and Wales, drew closer to their fellow Celts in Ireland and Brittany. There grew an appreciable activity along the routes across the Irish Sea to Cornwall and over to Brittany and the Continent, not only trade but the sending of churchmen from the better-organized monastic establishments to help their less fortunate brothers in Cornwall and elsewhere. One example was St Fimbarrus who in the sixth century, passing through on his way from Ireland to Rome,

Fowey. *(Edmund Swinglehurst)*

founded the church in Fowey which still bears his dedication. In this way the spark of Christianity was kept alive to survive in the west during the Dark Ages. On his return to his native land St Fimbarrus became the first bishop of Cork.

Then we have Castle Dore, just north of Fowey (see the legend of Tristan and Iseult, pp. 143–50), reputed to be the 'palace' of King Mark of Cornwall, and the ancient cross, now standing on the left of the A3082 as you enter Fowey, both on the line of this trackway.

Mention is made in the Domesday Book of manors in the Fowey area and shortly after the Norman Conquest Fowey became part of the possessions of the powerful Priory Tywardreath (between Fowey and St Austell), a daughter foundation of the Benedictine Abbey of Angers in France. Such a development would naturally strengthen Fowey's connections with France and the Continent. A breed of mariners was produced who spent their working lives in distant waters, even penetrating the Mediterranean.

Mingled with voyages of legitimate trade there were regrettably those of a less legitimate kind. Not satisfied with the dues collected from foreign trade the men of Fowey frequently engaged in piracy. Finding it difficult, no doubt, to control his flock from a distance and hoping to instil a sense of responsibility in its citizens, the Prior of Tywardreath in about 1200 granted Fowey a charter giving them a certain amount of control over their affairs. Whether or not he succeeded in his purpose, there is evidence that the Fowey fleet grew considerably. The sovereign had the right to call on ships and men for help in time of war and in 1264 Prince Edward, later Edward I, led 40 ships from Fowey against Simon de Montfort in the Channel. Some years later when he was King they were not so helpful and he tried to punish them for not having sent him assistance against the Scots.

Fowey men and ships did, however, figure prominently in the many wars of the Middle Ages. In 1346 they sent ships for the Crécy campaign and made the greatest contribution in ships and men for the later siege of Calais. In 1415 100 archers sailed from Fowey to fight in Agincourt. Unfortunately, when hostilities were supposed to cease and a truce was negotiated, the Fowey mariners either did not get the message or, if they had been told, chose to ignore the cease-fire. There are records of at least four occasions, in 1347, 1403, 1474 and 1486, when, usually as a result of complaints from abroad, the King was forced to take action against them for piracy and sometimes hanged the leaders. In the Wars of the Roses, Fowey supported the Earl of Warwick who owned land locally, but when the Earl was killed fighting against Edward IV, the King punished the town by removing the defensive chain that was stretched across the harbour and executing some leading citizens. The Earl must have helped build the present quite magnificent church in Fowey as his 'ragged staff' badge is carved on the west side of the fifteenth-century tower. A more reputable traffic of the town was the transport of pilgrims to the famous Shrine of St James of Compostela in Spain, many hundreds being carried in Fowey ships. Perhaps Chaucer's cheerful and much-married Wife of Bath passed through Fowey on her pilgrimage to Spain!

The Mistows (a corruption of Michaelstow – a hamlet just up the river from Fowey) were one of the foremost families combining piracy with normal trade, but the family with the longest history are the Treffrys who became lords of the manor in 1360 and who still occupy the castle-like manor house, Place, in the centre of the town. It was a Mistow who in 1403 captured a Spanish galleon when a truce was in force and in 1430 a rich Genoese vessel. Many reprisal raids were made in Fowey by both the French and Spanish.

There was much rivalry between Fowey and the Cinque Ports, so much so that Edward III in 1321 forbade Rye and Winchelsea to interfere with ships from Fowey and Polruan (opposite Fowey on the estuary). There was an instance when in answer to an insult from the Rye men the 'Fowey Gallants' gave them a good beating.

The Priory of Tywardreath was suppressed by Henry VIII and its estates taken over by the Treffry and Rashleigh families. The Rashleighs were related to Drake and Frobisher; John Rashleigh sailed with his ship *Frances of Fowey* on many of his cousins' expeditions and fought in the Armada. His town house is now the Ship Inn which in 1644 was the headquarters of the Earl of Essex, commander of the Parliamentary army. The Fowey folk were keen Royalists and the story is told of the Parliamentary fleet being frightened away by the women of the town who put on their red cloaks and armed with broomsticks paraded on the cliff-top. In the wars of the 1700s the call to man the ships impoverished the town and after the Napoleonic Wars the Fowey inhabitants turned once more to smuggling;

St Catherine's Castle, Fowey. *(Edmund Swinglehurst)*

even the Mayor, it was said, who only narrowly escaped detection.

In our own time the town has prospered, becoming a favourite yachting centre. Its appearance is not affected by the busy loading quay of the English China Clay Company farther up the river; in fact, the regular appearance of ocean-going vessels in the estuary enhances the interest of the little town.

One of our Walks takes us through the Menabilly Estate, lying in a lovely setting at the head of a wooded valley sloping down to the sea to the west of Fowey. This was the seat of the Rashleigh family for 300 years or more. In the time of the Civil War Jonathan Rashleigh complained that the Commonwealth troops had utterly wrecked his home and stripped it of everything of value. It is not known if he obtained redress after the Restoration; very likely not. In recent years it became the home of Daphne du Maurier, the novelist. Those who have read *Rebecca* are not likely to forget the dramatic opening lines 'Last night I dreamed I went back to Manderley' or the tensions of the story. Menabilly ('Manderley') provided the setting for *Rebecca*.

THE WALK:
FROM FOWEY, A CIRCULAR WALK VIA ST CATHERINE'S CASTLE, THE COAST, POLRIDMOUTH AND MENABILLY

MAP SQUARE D6
O.S. reference: 200/122516
A 2-hour circular walk.
Not suitable for Under Eights, as the path is near the cliff edge in parts.
Opportunity for a swim.
Take your own food and drink with you.

Fowey is reached by the A3082 which turns south-east off the A390 between St Austell and Lostwithiel. There is no parking in the narrow streets of Fowey and, for the purposes of this walk, it is preferable to use the large car park above the town: follow the sign TO CAR AND COACH PARK on the right as you enter Fowey by the A3082. (There is also a car park on the other side of the town near the Bodinnick Ferry but this would add quite a distance to the Walk.)

For the Walk, turn right out of the car park, cross the road and take the first turning on the left (Pikes Hill) which descends steeply. Bear right (not down St Finbarrow's Road) and drop down Dagland Road behind the Fowey Hotel. You come to the Esplanade running parallel to and with fine views of the estuary. Turn right along the Esplanade and after ½-mile you arrive at the delightful Readymoney Cove and tiny beach. On the right-hand side of a white cottage in front of you, you will see a path by a small spring and a COAST PATH sign. Follow the COAST PATH signs up through the woods and you reach a kissing-gate on to a path along the seaward edge of a field. Below you on the left are the ruins of a blockhouse built by the Treffrys and the citizens of Fowey in Henry VIII's time against possible invasion from France. The remains of a similar defence can be seen at Polruan the other side of the estuary. To your right on the hill is the nineteenth-century mausoleum of the Rashleigh family; adjoining the Castle site is that of the chapel of St Catherine erected in 1390 by Richard Mighelstow (Mistow), a member of that famous family who on this occasion instead of piracy adopted a more pious activity; there is also a record of his letting one of his ships on hire to the Black Prince for £20 for one of his campaigns. In the chapel – which gave the name to the adjacent headland – monks kept a light to guide mariners.

The Coast Path follows closely the edge of the cliff, descending steeply to two small patches of woodland (slippery in wet weather), down to Polridmouth (pronounced 'Pridmouth') Cove, a lovely spot, backed by a shining fresh-water lake. The beach is just right for a picnic or a swim. This is the bay in Daphne du Maurier's novel where Rebecca was drowned in her boat. It looks quiet enough in calm weather but can be treacherous in fog or rough weather. One of the sad wrecks here was that in

1856 of the Endeavour *from which only one of the crew was saved. This prompted the purchase by the Fowey community of a lifeboat, the successor of which can be seen at anchor in the harbour.*

To return to the car park by a different route from the outward one, take the path which leads up through the metal six-bar gate on the right-hand (east) side of the lake. This takes you over a stile and through woods and gorse. When the track seems to end, turn sharp right and climb the slope, hugging the boundary wall, keeping it on your right. When you reach the field-wall in front of you, turn left along its length; after about 100 yards you will come to an opening on your right with a concrete stile. Look back from the stile over the densely wooded valley. The house of Menabilly is there, hidden among the trees. Cross the stile on to the farm track; follow this and it will bring you out on to a road. Keep straight on and when you come to a fork turn right down Lankelly Lane. This will bring you to the main A3082. Turn right into the main road and continue down this until you reach a turning on the right opposite a telephone box. Take this road through the estate, on the far side of which you will find the car park.

For those with cars who do not want a long walk there is a shorter way down to Polridmouth Cove. As you leave Par on the A3082 on the way to Fowey you will see a signpost on the left, halfway up the hill, TO POLKERRIS AND MENABILLY. Turn right down this narrow road, keeping straight on until you reach the end with Menabilly Farm in front of you. On the right is a field car park. Continue on foot down the farm track past the farm and this will bring you after about 15 minutes to Polridmouth Cove.

Once at Polridmouth Cove energetic walkers may want to climb the field path leading from the Cove up to the Gribbin, the promontory crowned with the prominent red-and-white-striped 80-ft 'day-mark', erected, as the inscription tells us, by Trinity House in 1832. The headland, in common with most of the ground covered by this Walk, is owned by the National Trust and is noted for its fine views and some quite rare plant life. The climb to the Gribbin and down again will add about 1¼ miles to your walk. Allow 30 minutes each way.

There is a good daily bus service between St Austell and Fowey. St Austell is linked by bus and train with most centres in Cornwall.

2. THE HALL WALK

Charles the First's Narrow Escape

The year 1642 was a fateful one for the West Country as well as for the rest of the Kingdom. In July of that year there were the first armed clashes of the Civil War.

The Cornishmen followed, on the whole, the leading families of the county in supporting King Charles whereas Devon and Somerset were more for Parliament. Cornwall was to lose many brave men in this seven years' struggle that ended with victory for Cromwell.

By 1644 the Cornish Royalists had reason to be proud: early in the War they had routed the Parliamentarians, firstly at Braddock Down near Lostwithiel and later at Stratton near Bude. In July 1643 they won a great, though costly, victory at Bristol; a year later, the Parliamentary General, the Earl of Essex, after trying unsuccessfully to prevent the escape from Exeter of Queen Henrietta Maria, was trapped with 10,000 men, by the King's forces between Fowey and St Blazey.

Essex made his headquarters at what is now the Ship Inn at Fowey and sent for men and arms to help break out of the siege, but the Royalists prevented the ships getting through. The King himself was staying at Boconnoc near Lostwithiel (the pew used by the King in Boconnoc Church can be seen) and on August 17th, 1644, was walking with some of his officers along what is known as the Hall Walk, on the opposite bank of the River Fowey, observing the besieged enemy. The Hall Walk, named after the former seat of the Mohun family nearby, runs high above the river for 4 miles from Bodinnick, following the Pont Pill inlet and on to Polruan, connected by ferry with Fowey. As early as 1602 the traveller Carew mentioned what a pleasant walk it was.

Bodinnick – start of Hall Walk. *(Edmund Swinglehurst)*

As Charles and his entourage moved slowly along, a shot rang out and a young fisherman who was standing where the King had been a few moments before, fell dead, having been killed instantly by the bullet. There is no record of Charles's reaction but he probably took it as a sign that Providence was on his side. The siege was, in fact, soon over. As their position seemed hopeless the Parliamentarians surrendered on September 2nd but only after 2000 of their cavalry had two days earlier, cleverly taking advantage of misty and rainy weather, broken out at night. Essex was able to escape by boat.

The 6000 infantrymen prisoners were marched to Poole. They were badly treated en route – the Cornish took their revenge for what they thought was the harsh treatment they had suffered earlier from the Parliament troops when they entered the county. Out of the 6000, only 1000 reached Poole.

In 1646 the tables were turned and the Royalists had to give up almost all of Cornwall to Cromwell's General Fairfax.

For most of the details of the story of Fowey I am indebted to the booklet *Fowey. A brief history* by I. D. Spreadbury, BA, which contains a host of interesting facts and which I strongly recommend to those who would like to know more.

THE WALK:	MAP SQUARE D6
BY FERRY FROM FOWEY TO BODINNICK AND THEN BY THE HALL WALK TO POLRUAN; FERRY TO FOWEY	O.S. reference: 200/129522 Allow 2½ hours for the walk. Suitable for all ages. Muddy in places in wet weather. Good spots en route for picnics.

A frequent car-ferry service runs between Fowey and Bodinnick but as there is no car park in Bodinnick you should not take your car over but use the large car park at the Fowey end of the ferry – get there before 9.30 a.m. as it gets very full in the season. As you

Fowey – from Hall Walk. *(Edmund Swinglehurst)*

sail across the river you may ponder the fact that a ferry has been running there for 600 years at least.

Walk up the steep village street leading from the ferry. Have your camera ready as it makes one of the most charming pictures in south Cornwall. Near the top of the slope on the right-hand side of the street, is the entrance to a path, with a National Trust sign, between two stone walls. This is the start of the Hall Walk, with its fine views, for the whole of its 4 miles, of the woods and waters of the Fowey and Pont Pill estuaries. You will soon come across two monuments: one to the donor of the land and the other to Sir Arthur Quiller-Couch ('Q'), well-known Cornish author and former resident of Fowey. There is also a tablet commemorating King Charles' narrow escape.

When you pass through Pont, the hamlet at the head of the Pont Pill inlet whose few cottages among the woods delight the eye, you have to take to the road on the right for ½-mile (walk in single file facing oncoming traffic). Watch out for the continuation of the path on the right of the road near the top of the rise – it is well marked. You will eventually arrive at Polruan, another of Cornwall's old fishing villages. From Polruan there is a frequent passenger-ferry service to Fowey.

From the ferry terminal on the Fowey Esplanade, to reach the Bodinnick ferry car park you walk through the streets of old Fowey. Places of interest to look out for: fifteenth-century parish church; the Ship Inn (sixteenth-century town house of the Rashleigh family); and the most unusual Noah's Ark house in Fore Street dating from the fifteenth century – it is now an art shop which also contains a folk museum (admittance charge).

There are no refreshment facilities apart from the pubs at Bodinnick and Polruan.

THE SPECTRAL COACH

Those who know Looe and the south-east corner of Cornwall will be familiar with Talland Bay and have probably visited the fine old thirteenth-century Talland Church – the village itself seems to have disappeared from the map. In the early part of the eighteenth century the Vicar of Talland, the Reverend Mr Doidge, was very well known throughout the county not only for his learning but also as an exorcist; through his ministry many a ghost had been laid and many a family had found welcome relief from the unbearable strain of having spirits playing tricks in their homes.

One day in 1731 the Vicar of Talland had a message from a friend, the Rector of Lanreath, about 3 miles to the north-west. He told of mysterious happenings on the nearby Bocaddon Moor where local travellers had reported that when crossing the loneliest stretch they had suddenly encountered a fearful apparition: a black carriage, drawn by two headless black horses breathing flames from their nostrils, and driven by a screaming and shouting driver in black. The Lanreath Rector ventured an explanation that the ghostly driver could be the spirit of a local landowner who had been in a life-long dispute with a neighbour over a parcel of land on Bocaddon Moor which so preyed on his mind that he lost his reason, bringing him to an early death. He added that the whole matter was causing so much distress in the parish that he wondered if his friend could perhaps help.

Mr Doidge answered at once suggesting that they should investigate together the phenomenon and a meeting was arranged. They met just before midnight at the summit of the Moor on a dark night with a strong wind sending the clouds scudding from the west. The two clerics waited on their horses for an hour, seeing nothing unusual. They then walked their horses in a circle for half-an-hour or so with the same lack of result. Deciding their mission was a fruitless one they decided to go back home.

Mr Doidge had gone less than a mile on his homeward way when his horse began to behave in a strange and violent way. With ears laid back and snorting, it stopped short and then veered away from the track despite the efforts of its rider with spur and whip to bring it back. It appeared terrified. Doidge finally forced it round and, suspecting something unusual was occurring, galloped back to the summit of the Moor. He was horrified to see his friend stretched on the ground and, bending over him, a black figure who was holding the reins of two headless horses which were harnessed to a carriage. Doidge leaped from his horse and drawing out from his pocket the crucifix he always carried with him he held it towards the apparition and pronounced the words of the Church's exorcism rite. A scream came from the spectre and it and the horses and carriage vanished with a sound like rushing wind.

Doidge gave his friend (who was semi-conscious) a drink from his flask and helped him on to his horse, and leading it set off for Lanreath. Halfway they met a knot of villagers who with lanterns and staves were climbing the Moor to see what had happened. Apparently the Rector's riderless horse had galloped, sweating with fear, back to the village and the rectory stables. The villagers were roused and set out to search for the clergyman. The Rector recounted how the spectral coach and its driver had suddenly appeared from behind him as he was on his way home. His horse threw him and then bolted. He lost consciousness and knew nothing more until Mr Doidge tended him on the ground. It was obvious that he had received a profound shock and it was some days before he could resume his normal duties.

The spectral coach was never seen again.

THE WALK:
FROM PORTHALLOW
(TALLAND BAY) TO
TALLAND CHURCH

MAP SQUARE D6
O.S. reference: 201/224516
A short footpath climb to Talland Church, suitable for all ages. Allow 20 minutes each way.

Porthallow (Talland Bay) lies between West Looe and Polperro and is reached by a narrow road off the A387 which connects these resorts. There are two car parks – much in demand during the season so get there early – and cafés for teas and refreshments. The Coast Path passes through Porthallow. From the exits of the car parks follow the road eastwards for a short way and above Talland Bay beach you will see a COAST PATH sign and a kissing-gate. Go through the kissing-gate but instead of following the Coast Path along the edge of the cliff, turn left up the steep grass path. After a short, stiff climb you will come to a stile in the stone wall of the cemetery surrounding Talland Church.

In addition to being the church of which the Reverend Doidge was vicar, the building has much of interest. The separate tower is unusual and you will see in the porch some ancient stocks where they kept petty offenders as a punishment. The oldest parts of the church go back to the thirteenth century; the bench ends of the pews are beautifully carved – the workmanship dating from the 1600s. There are also some fine memorials and grave slabs carved in slate. On the south wall of the church is a list of rectors from the year 1264. Among them will be seen the name of the Reverend Richard Doidge who was vicar from 1713 to 1747. The excellent little guide on sale in the church confirms 'he was said to have the power to drive out devils' and was also thought to have been a bit of a smuggler on the side.

You can return the same way down the field path, giving you fine views of the coast. The beaches and rocks at Porthallow and Talland Bay are fine for children.

DANDO AND HIS DOGS

Just behind the magnificent church of St Germans is the site of the old Priory and the central figure of this tale is one of the Priory's monks who did not live up to his vows. Dando was a good-natured man and was generally liked by the St Germans folk, although he was unable to give them the spiritual guidance of which from time to time they were in need. It was not so much that he was fond of the good things of life such as food and strong ale, but he had one dominating passion and that was the hunt. Whatever the weather, whatever the day, Sundays, Saints' Days or other Feasts of the Church, if there was a chance of sport Dando was off on his horse with his pack of hounds either on his own or with his chosen companions, who were definitely not of a religious background, chasing whatever game was available. Hares were the main quarry as they were plentiful and not only provided excellent sport but made a tasty dish for supper.

The villagers watched with foreboding and told each other that no good would come of this. The Devil was sure to be on the lookout for him, and how right they were.

One Sunday, on which 'a southerly wind and a cloudy sky' gave promise of an excellent scent, Dando was up at daybreak, chivying his servants to get his horse saddled and the hounds ready. Off they dashed inland where they could cross the River Tiddy and then over the Lynher and down to Erth Barton, the ancient farm on Erth Hill which was the hunt's rendezvous that day.

His friends were all there and soon the hunt was in full cry on the open country surrounding the hill. Horses, riders and hounds were kept at full stretch well into the afternoon. Several hares were put up and as, on the few occasions when a short halt had to be made, heavy pulls at the pocket flasks were imperative, a jovial atmosphere was created to which friend Dando more than fully contributed. At last, as the light was failing and the time had come for a halt to be called, Dando was shattered to find there was not one drop left in his flask. 'Who's going to give me a drink?' he roared tipsily. 'My throat's a lime-kiln!' But his companions were in the same predicament and either had no liquor left or were so parched that they needed every drop for themselves. 'The Devil take you!' shouted Dando. 'I'd go to hell for a dram if the Devil would promise me one!' Just at that moment a sombrely dressed but splendidly horsed rider (who hadn't been noticed before) pushed himself forward and offered Dando a silver flask sparkling with inlaid jewels saying: 'Have a drink of this. I guarantee it will be to your taste.' Dando snatched it avidly and took a long drink. 'Where did you get this delectable brew?' he asked. 'Drink deep,' said the stranger. 'I've another flask here.' Dando drained the flask. 'I've never tasted such stuff,' he said. 'I'd give my life for such as this. What can I give you for it?' 'I'll take your hares,' answered the horseman, snatching the hares hanging on Dando's saddle-bow and spurring his horse down the slope. 'The devil you will,' shouted Dando and turning his horse and swaying in his seat, gave chase at full pelt after him, crying to the hounds to bring him down.

On they went at an infernal speed until they came to the bank of the Lynher where the stranger who, of course, was the Devil himself, took his horse in a gigantic leap far out into the stream. Dando and the hounds, in full cry, followed and all – horse, rider and hounds – disappeared with an almighty splash below the surface from which arose a cloud of hissing steam.

Dando was never seen again. When the other riders returned to their homes and told of the day's terrible happening a sense of fear filled the souls of everyone. It is said that the lesson was taken very much to heart by the monks of the Priory and the inhabitants of St Germans. Many made gifts of money to the church in the hope that they might escape the dreadful fate of Dando. When you visit the church you will find, on the right-hand side (south) of the nave, in the far corner near the chancel, the story of Dando and his dogs carved on a 'miserere' or choir seat. This is from part of the earlier fourteenth-century choir of the Priory which was destroyed after the Dissolution of the Monasteries. You will see Dando with his crossbow and his dogs on their last hunt.

THE WALK:
A SHORT WALK FROM
ST GERMANS CHURCH
ALONG THE BANK OF THE
RIVER

MAP SQUARE E6
O.S. reference: 201/359578
A pleasant 20-minute stroll, suitable for all ages.

St Germans is situated a few miles inland from the coast between Looe and Plymouth and can be reached via the A387 from Looe or the A374 from Liskeard. The village, dominated by one of the largest and most beautiful churches of the south-west in a lovely setting, is well worth a visit. St Germans was the seat of the Saxon Bishops of Cornwall from AD 930 to 1043 when Cornwall was absorbed into the See of Exeter. Until 1876, when the Bishopric of Cornwall was reinstated with the seat at Truro, St Germans was regarded by the Cornish as their 'Cathedral'. The church is bounded on the north by the site of the former Augustinian Priory, founded in the twelfth century. After the Dissolution of the Monasteries the Priory was bought by the Eliot family, the Earls of St Germans, who built their present seat, Port Eliot House, in the eighteenth century. The house and grounds can be glimpsed behind the church and help to form the perfect setting (the house is not open to the public).

St Germans Church has some splendid Norman features and you can buy inside an illustrated guide with details of its structure and its fascinating 1000-year history. After visiting the church and seeing the Dando wood-carving, return to the main road and turn left. Where the road curves to the right after a few yards, keep straight on down the lane which borders the St Germans Estate. On the right, 300 yards down this lane, is the start of a path, with a PUBLIC FOOTPATH sign. Take this path, which runs along the edge of a field. The path then enters a wood and goes under the arches of the railway viaduct, emerging on the bank of the estuary of the River Tiddy, with a small sailing station, St Germans Quay, and some charming cottages.

Ahead of you, to your left, you will see the rising ground on the left bank of the River Lynher which joins the Tiddy below the Quay. This is Erth Hill down which Dando and his dogs, pursuing the Devil, dashed to their destruction. Continue up the road leading from the Quay and you come to the main road. Turn right, under the railway, and a few minutes' walk will bring you back to the church. There is a good pub, The Eliot Arms, farther up the road.

A Western National bus service connects Looe and Plymouth with St Germans. St Germans has a station on the Plymouth–Penzance main railway line but the service is infrequent.

BIBLIOGRAPHY

L. Alcock. *By South Cadbury that is Camelot*. Thames and Hudson. 1972.

G. Ashe. *King Arthur's Avalon*. Collins. 1957.

Hilaire Belloc. *The Romance of Tristan and Iseult*. George Allen. 1903.

R. D. Blackmore. *Lorna Doone*. 1869.

Piers Brendon. *Hawker of Morwenstow*. Cape. 1975.

M. Coate. *Cornwall in the Great Civil War and Interregnum*. Clarendon Press. 1933.

Cornwall Archaeological Society. *Field Guide 2. Principal Antiquities of the Land's End District*.

E. M. R. Ditmas. *Tristan and Iseult in Cornwall*. Forrester Roberts. 1969.

R. Gittings. *The Older Hardy*. Heinemann. 1978.

R. Gittings. *Young Thomas Hardy*. Heinemann. 1975.

Thomas Hardy. *A Pair of Blue Eyes*. 1873.

R. Hunt. *Popular Romances of the West of England*. 1881.

M. Raine. *The Wars of the Roses*. Wheaton. 1968.

A. L. Rowse. *Tudor Cornwall*. Macmillan. 1969.

Alfred, Lord Tennyson. *Idylls of the King*. 1872.

R. F. Treherne. *The Glastonbury Legends*. Cresset Press. 1967.

C. V. Wedgwood. *The King's War 1641–47*. Collins. 1958.

The author gratefully acknowledges permission from the Oxford University Press for the quotation of part of the poem 'Song' by Sidney Godolphin from the *Oxford Book of 17th Century Verse*, also for the verse from *Cornwall in the Great Civil War and Interregnum* by Mary Coate. He also gratefully acknowledges the permission from Macmillan Administration for the quotation from 'Under the Waterfall' from the *Collected Poems of Thomas Hardy*.

Assistance from the staffs of the Public Libraries of Croydon and Truro has been invaluable and the author gratefully acknowledges this.

The photographs on pp. 87, 88 are by courtesy of West Country Tourist Board. The photograph on page 30 is reproduced by permission of the Exmoor National Park Dept. Other photographs are by Edmund Swinglehurst.

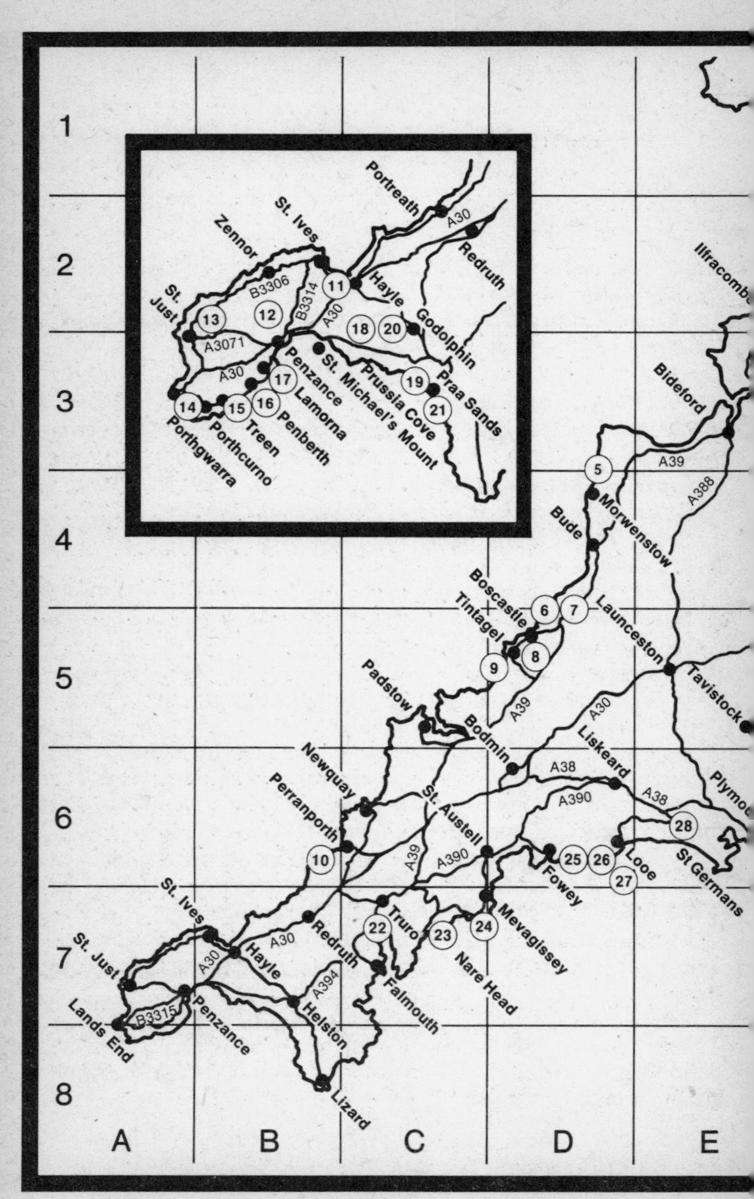

1
2
3
4
5
6
7
8
A
B
C
D
E
Portreath
St. Ives
Zennor
A30
Redruth
B3306
B3314
Hayle
St. Just
A30
Godolphin
A3071
Penzance
St. Michael's Mount
Prussia Cove
Praa Sands
A30
Lamorna
Penberth
Treen
Porthcurno
Porthgwarra
Ilfracombe
Bideford
A39
A388
Bude
Morwenstow
Boscastle
Tintagel
Launceston
Tavistock
Padstow
A39
A30
Bodmin
Liskeard
Newquay
A38
A390
A38
Perranporth
St. Austell
Plymouth
A39
A390
Fowey
Looe
St Germans
St. Ives
Mevagissey
Truro
St. Just
A30
Redruth
Hayle
A30
A394
Nare Head
Falmouth
Penzance
B3315
Lands End
Helston
Lizard

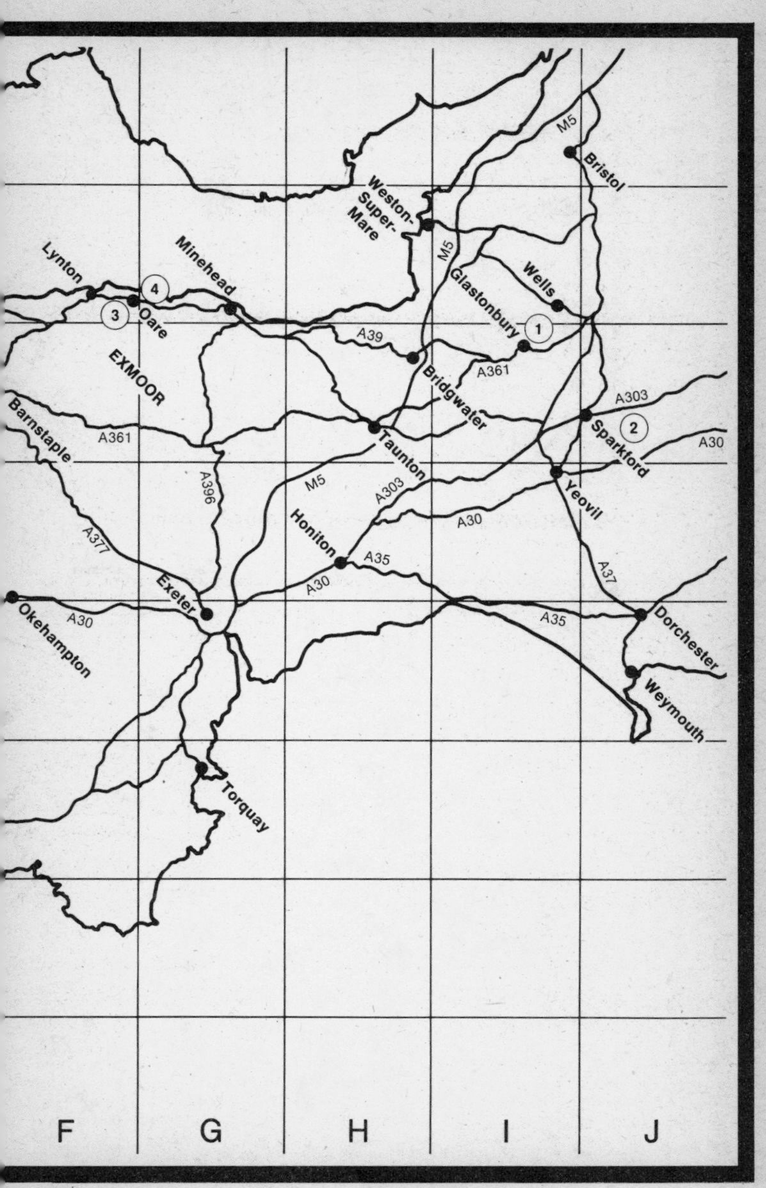

Bristol
M5
Weston-
Super-
Mare
M5
Wells
Glastonbury
1
Lynton
Minehead
4
3
Oare
A39
Bridgwater
A361
EXMOOR
A303
2
Sparkford
A30
Barnstaple
A361
Taunton
M5
A396
A303
Yeovil
A30
Honiton
A377
A35
A37
Exeter
A30
Okehampton
A30
A35
Dorchester
Weymouth
Torquay
F
G
H
I
J

KEY TO REFERENCE MAP

THE FEARFUL VOID Geoffrey Moorhouse £1.25
There is a fearful void out there in the empty quarter of the Sahara Desert, but more terrifying still is the void within our minds – the fear of loneliness and failure. One man's search to conquer his own self-distrust. Illustrated in full colour.

JOURNEY THROUGH BRITAIN John Hillaby £1.25
It was a magical idea to walk through the over-industrialized land of Britain from Land's End to John O'Groats, avoiding all centres of population. Britain's master walker made his reputation with this book. Illustrated.

JOURNEY THROUGH EUROPE John Hillaby £1.50
John Hillaby gives a splendid potpourri of factual account, lively anecdote, mythology and private comment in this account of his walk from the Hook of Holland via the Alps to Nice. Illustrated.

JOURNEY TO THE JADE SEA John Hillaby 95p
Tired of city-living and ashamed of his toleration of boredom, John Hillaby made a three-month safari from the Northern Frontier District of Kenya to the legendary Jade Sea. Illustrated.

JOURNEY THROUGH LOVE John Hillaby £1.25
Hillaby's most recent and possibly most powerful and evocative book concerns a series of several walks, in Yorkshire, Wales, London, the South Downs and North America, and the thread running through the narrative is the story of a great tragedy and loss.

A JOURNEY TO THE HEART OF ENGLAND
Caroline Hillier £1.50
A superbly informative and entertaining look at the towns, landscapes, industries and history of the Western Midlands, an area rich in tradition and very much the heart of England.

ENGLAND IN THE AGE OF HOGARTH
Derek Jarrett £1.50
An absorbing history which effectively debunks the traditionally cosy view of the eighteenth century as an age of elegance and freedom.

THE ENGLISH MEDIEVAL TOWN Colin Platt £2.25
The definitive study of the life, work, architecture and people of medieval England. Illustrated.

EUROPE'S INNER DEMONS Norman Cohn £1.75
The history of the vilification of minority groups as scapegoats, by the author of THE PURSUIT OF THE MILLENNIUM.

EVOLUTION OF THE HOUSE Stephen Gardiner £1.50
A history of dwelling places and domestic architecture from the cave onwards. Fully illustrated.

FOLK SONG IN ENGLAND A L Lloyd £1.50
The classic history of the natural expressions of the British people.

FOOD IN HISTORY Reay Tannahill £1.95
Man's real history in his search for food; the measure of civilization is man's attitude towards food. A vastly entertaining and authoritative panorama. Illustrated.

THE QUEST FOR ARTHUR'S BRITAIN
Geoffrey Ashe £1.75
The story of Arthur and the Knights of the Round Table, the chief myth of Britain. How true is it? Illustrated.

THE ROSICRUCIAN ENLIGHTENMENT
Frances A Yates £1.50
The Rosicrucians stood midway between the Dark Ages and the scientific Renaissance. The Hermetic tradition of magic, alchemy and the Kabbalah revealed.

RUSSIA IN REVOLUTION Lionel Kochan £1.75
A compact, readable and authoritative account of one of the most important events in modern history.

SHAKESPEARE THE MAN A L Rowse £1.25
The identity of the dark lady of the sonnets is revealed, and Shakespeare is set in the context of his friends, patrons and contemporaries – not merely of his plays.

THE SLOW BURNING FUSE John Quail £1.95
The activities, triumphs, disasters, influence and personalities of the anarchist movement; a history long neglected.

A HISTORY OF WESTERN MUSIC
Christopher Headington £1.95
A fully illustrated account of the development of song, opera, of various musical instruments, musicians and music itself.

MANKIND AND MOTHER EARTH
Arnold J Toynbee £3.50
Arnold Toynbee's last book – a one-volume history of civilization that is breathtaking in its scope, scholarship and imagination.

THE PALADIN HISTORY OF ENGLAND
A new nine-volume history of England from pre-Roman to modern times.

THE FORMATION OF ENGLAND
H P R Finberg £1.25
Part of the new Paladin History of England series. This volume deals with Britain in the Dark Ages between Roman and Norman conquests.

THE CRISIS OF IMPERIALISM Richard Shannon £1.25
England in the realm of Victoria. A time of development, expansion, colonization, enormous social upheavals and reform.

PEACE, PRINT AND PROTESTANTISM
C S L Davies £1.25
Third in the Paladin History of England series. C S L Davies' book deals with the period 1450–1558 encompassing the reign of the Tudors and the breakaway from the Church of Rome.

AFRICA IN HISTORY Basil Davidson £1.95
A complete introduction to the history of the 'Dark Continent'. Illustrated.